Guy's Guide to the Flipside

The Other Vancouver
by Guy Bennett

Photography by
Mandelbrot

ARSENAL PULP PRESS
VANCOUVER CANADA

GUY'S GUIDE TO THE FLIPSIDE
COPYRIGHT © 1992 GUY BENNETT

ARSENAL PULP PRESS LTD.
100-1062 Homer Street
Vancouver, B.C. V6B 2W9

Edited by Mary Schendlinger
Typeset by the Vancouver Desktop Publishing Centre
Printed and bound in Canada by Kromar Printing

CANADIAN CATALOGUING IN PUBLICATION DATA:
Bennett, Guy, 1959-
  Guy's guide to the flipside
  ISBN 0-88978-250-4
  1. Vancouver (B.C.)—Guidebooks. 2. Vancouver (B.C.)—Humor.
I. Title.   FC3847.18.B42 1992   917.11'33044   C92-091561-2
F1089.5.V22B45 1992

I would like to acknowledge my friends and relatives who helped me write this book: Wendy Atkinson, Sara Bennett, David Bloom, Alexa Fox, Piper Hart, Brian Lam, Steve Osborne, Mary Schendlinger, and the many people too numerous to mention who gave me support throughout the project. –G.B.

Contents

This book is dedicated to Tiger Williams:
"An asshole is an asshole whether he's a nuclear physicist or a hockey fan, and sometimes there is a big temptation to drive him one straight between the eyes."

Preface

When you set out to examine an organism you may take its pulse from a multitude of different positions. The same is true if the "organism" is a bar or a restaurant. In the beginning stages of researching this book I tested, and subsequently abandoned, a number of techniques (interviewing managers, tracing ownership, history, etc.) before discovering that the essence of the beast may be summoned by observing and documenting the behaviour of the patrons inside it.

In the last five years, some of the venues have shut down or changed so radically as to be unrecognizable. These will be noted to stop you wandering around looking for something that doesn't exist. Remember, it does *not* matter if you own the first version of this book—you'd be foolhardy not to get this one as well. The spelling mistakes have been corrected and there's a brand new chapter called "Skin." As I have discovered, all Triple X theatres are not created equal.

Guy's Guide to the Flipside is *virtually guaranteed* to effect positive change in your life. In the weeks following your purchase it would not be unreasonable to expect intensified lovemaking and favourable turns in the stock market; withdrawn adolescent offspring may reject the drug culture in favour of differential calculus.

You might have noticed that I have dedicated the book to Tiger Williams. For those of you who don't know, Tiger Williams was the son of a bully, a plucky little guy from a small town in the prairies who decided he wanted to play NHL hockey. Unfortunately his knees bent the wrong way and no matter how hard he worked, he couldn't skate very fast. But he

1100 BLOCK GRANVILLE STREET, SOUTH SIDE

still wanted to play hockey. So he became a brawler: he had to beat people up every day at work to keep his job. Tiger Williams is my favourite Canadian.

Food

There are enough restaurants in Vancouver to fill twenty books of this size. I chose the ones I did because they are unusually interesting, ugly, cheap, or beautiful. A plate of food is a very difficult thing to review. The more you get to know it, the more it disappears down your throat. Finally you are left staring stupidly at a dirty paper napkin, conscious of nothing but the waitress and the ticking of the clock. So, as a food critic, I had big performance anxieties, and often found myself drifting to the washroom where it's all trickles and gurgles and the odd scrotum tangled cruelly in the metal zipper teeth.

Somehow it doesn't feel quite right, bribing somebody to cook and serve my dinner. I know in my heart it's a task that should be performed by someone intimate, not these impoverished strangers, forcing a smile at the critical moments. It's like buying a woman for sex: there's an ingredient you can never get.

PENDER STREET, 100 BLOCK EAST, NORTH REAR

Jackson's Beef House

207 WEST HASTINGS

HOURS: MON–SAT: 7:00 A.M.–6 P.M.

PHONE: 681-3726

AVERAGE MEAL: $4.00

Located right across from Victory Square in the basement of the old Toronto Dominion Building, Jackson's Beef House is probably the most greasy spoon in the world. The long curving counters are framed by sunset murals of perky native girls doing perky things on the beach. There's a gridwork of ceiling pipes painted above my head.

The waitress is one of those rare people who seems to be happy exactly where she is: a bubbly middle-aged woman wearing just the right amount of make-up; an ex-traffic stopper carved in the old tradition of the big-hearted roadside waitress, so you feel a wave of warmth and safety when she slides the burger down in front of you.

The old man cooking in the back is actually the owner, Micky McGalos. He refuses to say how long he's owned the place— even the waitress isn't sure, but he figures since some time in the mid-sixties. Micky looks pretty burnt out. Like lots of old men, he doesn't seem to hear very well. When the waitress hollers that I am writing about the place, he looks very distrustful, so she adds, "—and he'll bring us lots and lots of customers!"

I order a clubhouse sandwich, which comes with fries and gravy. I can't wait to get it inside my stomach, but this waitress is so sweet I feel self-conscious chewing in front of her. Micky goes silently back to the kitchen. She says, "You wouldn't believe how hard he works back there, preparing homemade soup, fresh fish, roast beef and gravy. I know he doesn't seem friendly. He's an old man . . . he . . . well . . . he doesn't know what to say to you." He doesn't have to say anything to me. He is a silent old man and she sounds as if she is in love with him.

Little Spot Restaurant

33 EAST HASTINGS (LAST SEEN: 1989)
PHONE: 681-0624
HOURS: MON, TUES, WED, SAT: 7 A.M.–6 P.M.
AVERAGE MEAL: $3.50

Though hardly a meeting place for the beautiful people, the Little Spot can be depended on to serve a nutritious meal at a very reasonable price. Spaghetti with meat sauce, dinner soup and a bun, is $2.65. Jumbo muffins baked daily are 40 cents.

The main dining area is a study in controversial parenting techniques. You see the little ones sitting rigidly in clouds of secondary smoke, swatted occasionally for fingering the cutlery or laughing out loud while the big people are talking.

My only complaint with the Little Spot concerns the surly and untrusting attitude of the management toward the patrons. A crudely pencilled sign taped to the side of the cash register warns: "Do not ask for credit," while in the washrooms the toilet paper is actually padlocked into place—an economy which led one patron to discard his soiled underwear in a bucket in the corner.

Marine View Coffee Shop

103–611 ALEXANDER ST. (AS SEEN IN 1987—
AT ITS FORMER LOCATION ON CENTENNIAL)
HOURS: MON–FRI: 7 A.M.–3:30 P.M.
PHONE: 253-0616
AVERAGE MEAL: $5.00

The seagulls swarm and scream above me. Look out the window onto a battleground of commercial fishing boats. Through the white barn doors of Ocean Fisheries I see a cluster of black-haired women in rubber boots, hacking away at the wiggling salmon. The waitress has greasy brown hair and a ski-slope nose. She smiles at me weakly. My face is crammed full of delicious fresh fish and chips and I'm wired to the nuts on this coffee.

The picture outside is more seductive than a television screen. My faith in Canada is restored. A team of men in plastic pants stroll confidently across a floating dock. They are all wearing hard hats. One of them lies down on his belly. Reaching over the side of the dock, he starts pounding a metal spike, driving it into a floating log with the blunt end of an axe. It's like watching your only child play hockey, waiting for him to split his head open on the back stroke.

On the way to the washroom I pass the biological branch of The Fisheries Research Board. There's no end of interesting stuff on the bulletin board, and I think perhaps a hint of scandal in this notice to the industry:

During the recent 4-day troll fishery which concluded on Friday, July 5, 1985, it is estimated that 27,300 pieces of chinook salmon were harvested. This figure is well in excess of the 12,000 pieces it was anticipated would be harvested during each of the three proposed 4-day fisheries in early July. As a result, in consultation with the troll representatives, the management strategy for the chinook fishery has now been

MAIN STREET

---

altered to ensure that the 50K ceiling, as set for the Strait of Georgia commercial troll fishery, will not be exceeded in 1987.

And right next to it, a unique idea for a stocking stuffer: it's a handsome MARCO WT-202 trawl winch with 1000-fathom (3/4" cable) drum capacity, complete with Webster Control Valve, Munson Tyson remote control, spare Vickers Motor and G1993 Gearbox, all for $20,000.

The couple sitting beside me are speaking German. I can't understand a word. The man is one of these intense fidgety guys, incapable of saying anything in an offhand way. A bit of English sneaking into the conversation. In a very grandiose manner the man asks, "Would you like some oysters?" and the woman says, "Oh yes!" and then makes a frantic gesture for him to keep his voice down when she sees me watching. They go back to speaking German. I've got to stop watching married people or I'll never do it myself.

Tread carefully down the slippery wooden dock. Tip-toe past a severed seagull wing and a blood-smeared tampon. The fishermen stare at me as the cold wind tears at my face. By some fluke of reflection the houses on the North Shore are glittering like flakes of gold.

The Only Seafoods Cafe

20 EAST HASTINGS

HOURS: NOON–7.00 P.M.

PHONE: 681-6546

AVERAGE MEAL: $10.00

A man is knocked down in the middle of the intersection and a crowd of onlookers stand quiet and resolute as he disappears into the back of an ambulance. I have to sidestep a puddle of vomit and a mutilated pigeon just to sit in this horseshoe of ogres. I love this guy across from me. It's an anatomy lesson watching his jaw muscles flash up and down, and a physiology practicum in the body fluids that spew when he sneezes.

I don't mind spending $4.00 on a bowl of Coney Island Clam Chowder. All these lumpy bits make me feel healthy. There's a whole family eating halibut. When I point and ask the waitress, "Where does the halibut come from?" she gives me a look that says, "Why, the ocean, you asshole." I'll just spread mountains of butter on these hunks of fresh brown bread and ignore the people standing behind me waiting for a seat.

The soup'll keep me going all afternoon, but I won't come back here for a long time. It's worse than modern Russia. Lots of cold dirty people, with all the subtle romanticism of a Greyhound bus station.

Save-On-Meat Inc.

43 WEST HASTINGS
PHONE: 693-7761
HOURS: MON–SAT: 8:30 A.M.–6 P.M.
AVERAGE MEAL: $3.00

The neon arrows point me in off the street. I find myself dumbstruck by a blood-smeared blonde woman pushing hunks of pork through a "Butcher Boy" band saw. A guy in a white lab coat comes up behind her and places his hands on her waist. She smiles and waits until his hands are gone before she begins cutting again. Concentrating is the sexiest thing a blonde can do.

Here's a couple of fat fleshy fish chewing a stream of bubbles in a plastic bucket. A sign on the bucket says: "Live Carp $2.99/lb." They move around in lazy circles. I've seen women move like that at parties, and when they reach me I don't trust anything they say. On the other side of the glass there is a middle-aged Oriental woman, standing with her hands behind her back as if she's been hired to guard the fish. She says, "They're a kind of goldfish." I ask her, "If I buy one, will you kill it for me?" She steps back, as if this is a slightly impertinent question, and replies, "Yes, I'll hit it over the head for you if you want me to." Listen to all the foreign languages floating through the air.

I buy a chunk of sharp cheddar cheese and go sit in the cafeteria at the back. Here's a guy who looks like Abe Lincoln coming off a drunk, but his table manners are perfect. He keeps dabbing the sides of his mouth with a paper napkin and pushing his fists into the sockets of his eyes. The waitress hovers over a Native boy, about thirteen years old, who is squinting into the menu. Five minutes later he puts the menu down and orders a root beer, turns to me with an innocent smile and says, "I'm waiting here for my mother."

The washroom in the back is so dark you could hide a body there. As my eyes adjust, I can make out the cartoon face of a bald man with missing teeth. A balloon coming out the side of his head says, "The only thing wrong with dope is that it wears off." The

4110 MAIN STREET

Indian kid finishes his root beer and leaves without his mother.
I buy a pork chop from the blonde girl. She wraps it up in white
paper and smiles at me as she hands it over. There's blood on
her apron. Simple politeness is so moving. I can feel that smile
bouncing around inside me somewhere.

White Lunch Cafeteria

124 WEST HASTINGS (LAST SEEN: 1987)
HOURS: 7 A.M.–11 P.M.
PHONE: 689-5356
AVERAGE MEAL: $4.00

Slide my tray along these metal railings past the doughnuts and the wedges of lemon pie. Stainless steel buckets full of chicken and chili and steamed vegetables. I don't care if it is 4 o'clock in the afternoon, I feel like breakfast. Two eggs, 2 slices of toast, hash browns and 3 pieces of bacon for $2.00.

There's room in this booth to spread a newspaper out and thrash my feet around under the table. The light doesn't hurt my eyes the way it does at McDonald's, although I miss the Leggo and the floating toys. This is a perfect breakfast. As good as Mom could make it. Dump so much cream in the coffee it tastes smooth.

Look at this wobbly old geezer in the gangster suit ordering 3 Ukrainian sausages, mashed potatoes, carrots, peas, and french fries. After the plate is stacked with food he points at it and requests a hypothetical subtotal based on the premise that one of the Ukrainian sausages is missing. The Oriental woman is very patient with him, gently removing one sausage and loading on extra carrots instead.

Here's a teenage girl in a track suit. Great big hips like after childbirth. She selects a chunk of lemon pie and a glass of coke. Since I'm full of courage I'll sit down beside her and try some of that small conversation. I know it's a hit and miss thing.

GUY: Hi, how are you doing?

GIRL: Okay I guess.

GUY: How's the pie?

GIRL: It's okay.

GUY: How's the Coke?

GIRL: It's all right.

GUY: Would you say it's fizzy?

73 WEST HASTINGS STREET REAR

GIRL: I guess.

GUY: Would you say it tastes like normal Coke?

GIRL: Listen, I don't want to be rude, but could you, like, leave? I'd rather be alone.

GUY: Watch me. I'm disappearing.

Clark Gable I'm obviously not. Never mind, there's Bruce Springsteen walking right into The White Lunch Cafeteria with his leather jacket and bandana, ordering coffee to go. He looks even shorter than he does in the videos. I can't believe nobody else has recognized him. Wipe the toast away and stumble up to the counter, holding out my hand and saying, "I love *Nebraska*"—have the little guy turn to me: "So do I, Schmuck, but I'm not Bruce Springsteen." Well why be such an asshole as to go around looking like him?

Retreat to the washroom and wash away the humiliation with handfuls of clear warm water. You know, I don't appreciate the crude illustration of homosexual domesticity above the sink, or the smell of piss in the air.

Wo Fat & Co.

30 EAST HASTINGS (LAST SEEN: CIRCA 1988)
BLACK BEAN CAKE: $.60

I would never have known about this place if it weren't for my childhood friend David Bloom, who called me up after a winter of sitting around the West End doing MDA with his teenage girlfriend. He said, "We're all connected," and I said, "Why don't we meet downtown for a cup of tea?"

The Wo Fat is a one-room Chinese cake factory which has occupied the same position on Hastings Street since the 1920s. Although the bulk of their business is done selling wholesale to restaurants Canada-wide, you can walk in off the street and buy a single cake at a time. You'll see a tall Oriental man hunched over the ovens in the back of the shop. Particularly recommended are the Almond Cookies and the Black Bean Cakes, which sell for 30 cents and 60 cents respectively.

When David first took me into the shop, we ordered a couple of Black Bean Cakes and we were standing around while a tiny Oriental woman, who is in fact the granddaughter of the original owner, wrapped them up for us. She placed the cakes on a glass display case that functions as a counter. Inside the case there was a bunch of old Chinese newspapers, assorted pens, a dirty drinking glass, and a dehydrated mandarin orange. I was in a phase where I was gaining confidence in my social skills and I felt compelled to interact with every bank teller, waitress and salesman I came in contact with. I pointed to the orange and said, "How much?" After a moment's confusion she shook her head vigorously, insisting that the orange was not for sale, even after I indicated I was willing to pay anything for it.

Next time I went in by myself. I bought a Black Bean Cake. The orange was still sitting in the display case, shrivelled up like an arctic testicle. I pointed my finger at it and said, "I would like to buy that orange." She took it out and let me touch it, but again, insisted that it was not for sale.

For the next three years, every time I walked into the Wo Fat she would greet me with an amused smile and we would talk

PENDER AND CARRALL

about the orange which had stabilized in a completely shrivelled state, retaining most of its colour. Sometimes we'd be rather coy, chatting about it as if it weren't important and then I'd inquire, very casually, how much the thing was worth. Always the same answer: sorry, not for sale.

I left town for a year. When I got back I went to the Wo Fat & Co. (not right away) and saw that the Oriental woman was still there, and the orange was gone. I felt sad watching her package the cakes. I said, "Where is my orange?" She broke into a gorgeous impish smile, like a naughty little girl who is too cute to be punished. She said, "I sold it."

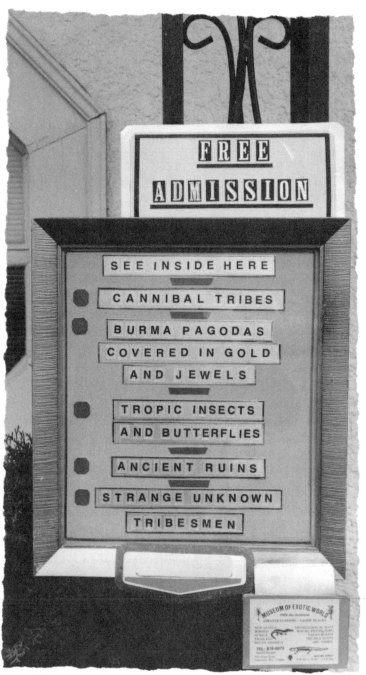

3651 MAIN STREET

Drink

In the spring of 1980 there was a teenage boy living in a cube-shaped apartment building with his pregnant girlfriend. He had a job repairing scaffolding. The girl was very much in love with him, very old-fashioned. Every night she cooked him a full-course meal, and afterwards he felt flattered and trapped.

He was hanging out with a couple of strippers from the east, drinking with them after work, never touching them or making love to them. The strippers thought it was the strangest thing in the world that he was going to be a father. They told him it would never work.

He worked hard at the scaffolding shop, as if by working he could somehow generate a solution to the rest of his life. Their baby girl was born one month premature. She looked like a red monkey. She lived in an incubator for the first two weeks of her life, cried most of the time. They could only touch her with rubber gloves on.

The baby came home. The boy spent more time there, but he was restless amidst the baby's constant screaming and the pervading sweet-sour smell of her shit. The girl was less in love with him. She said, "In my wildest dreams, I never dreamt you could be so cold." They argued constantly, without passion. The girl took the baby and retreated back into the country to live with her mother. An ex-biker moved into her room. He was a filthy pig, but an excellent cook.

The scaffolding company offered to send the boy to welding school. He jumped at the chance, but quickly established himself as a daydreamer, so that after a week the head of the welding department called him into the office, told him he was a slack bastard and he'd better pull up his socks or hit the road.

He went back to the apartment and lay down on his bed. The baby girl had her own teeth now. She was crawling. He thought of quitting welding school. It was only the startling lack of alternatives that persuaded him to press on. The ex-biker cooked prawns in lemon, garlic and butter. They ate together quietly, washing the food down with cans of warm beer. After dinner the boy listened to an account of a gangbang, involving a menstruating woman in a garage, many years before.

The boy climbed into his leather jacket and went downtown to drink. Drinking, as always, to get drunk.

In a bar he met a large woman draped in a loose brown cotton dress. She had substantial sagging breasts, a swelling belly, the kind of loud hoarse laugh you frequently find in good-hearted people who drink a good deal—a hippie woman tottering nervously at the top of the long downslide into middle age.

She introduced the boy to the table of friends. They were all men. One of them was supposed to be her boyfriend. His name was Chico. Chico nodded his head, never said anything.

Later the boy felt his balls being massaged under the table. The hippie woman said, "I made love to an eleven-year-old boy once—my best friend's kid." She said, "Take this," and pushed something soft into his lap. It was Chico's hat.

The American Hotel

928 MAIN STREET (AS SEEN IN 1989—MOST
OF THE BIKER CROWD HAVE GRAVITATED TO
THE CALIFORNIA ON GRANVILLE)
PHONE: 681-5839

This is biker territory and it's an excellent place to get beaten up. To attract attention, make long-term enemies, and save time parking, plough your trusty Japanese import into the row of shining Harley Davidsons out front. With an impact velocity of around 85 km/h and the correct angle, you should be able to get most of them. If you want to be a living legend, all you have to is climb out of your car and run away. If you want to be a dead legend, stroll in and break the news gently. "Guess what silly old me's gone and done," might work as well as anything else.

Here's a tall leather-clad blonde woman propped against the bar, so close I can feel her breath. She pulls out a cigarette. There's practically a riot, all the guys wanting to light it. I like tall blondes myself, but listen here young lady, blowing smoke rings like that is nothing short of criminal. And look at the big scruffy hippie stumbling towards her. Wiping the foam from his moustache and leaning right into her ear. She laughs like this guy is so funny he should have his own show. He drops his hand onto the curve of her ass. She tilts her head back so you can see the whole length of her smooth white throat. And now there's danger. Even I can smell it. The hippie gets a couple of fingers dug up into the crevice of her ass. She jumps and slaps him, and a huge tattooed monster steps out of the shadows, turns the hippie around and punches him three times in the head. As the hippie falls he is kicked again in the windpipe. The woman drains her beer. Her face is strangely contorted as if she is submitting to anal intercourse.

The American is heating up with the sounds of Innuendo, an excellent blues/rock band, featuring guitar wizard Robbie Montgomery and singer/harp player Sherman Tank.

23

684 EAST HASTINGS STREET

Montgomery flings the guitar behind his neck Hendrix-style, unleashing a flurry of stinging hot licks. A couple of girls jump onto the stage to dance. They don't look old enough to drink.

During a break between sets a young woman with beautiful dreamy eyes walks onto the dance floor and exposes her breasts. The bouncer leads her away by the elbow, and they both smile as if it is a joke they just can't get tired of.

I like the American because everything I prize about myself is absolutely worthless here.

Arlington Cabaret

1236 WEST BROADWAY (REPLACED BY THE
BIG BAM BOO IN 1990); PHONE: 733-2220
HOURS: MON–THU: 7 P.M.–1 A.M; FRI–SAT: 7
P.M.–2:30 A.M; SUN: 7 P.M.–MIDNIGHT

Step right off Broadway and up a flight of wooden steps into the early fifties. Red tablecloths, balloons, lots of old folks waltzing across the pine dance floor. Sit with the other single guys against the back wall. It's good advertising not to let my shoulders droop.

At the door the woman said I didn't have to pay since it was so late. Her face was jaundiced and her eyes were unfashionably baggy. She looked calm, almost relieved.

I'm sure these people graduated from Arthur Murray's. They count themselves in, and the way they're running around trading partners I think this is thinly disguised wife-swapping. I'd like to go for a spin around the dance floor myself, but all the old guys would be pissed off because I don't have a wife of my own to chip in.

Without a doubt this is the best Latino ballroom music I've ever heard. I've forgotten all about my troubles. The band consists of a guitarist, an accordion player, and a drummer. The guitarist looks like an aging Cuban soccer player. He puts his guitar down and walks off to the bar in the middle of a song. The other two follow him with their eyes. They pick up the tempo. They sound better without him.

Out on the dance floor, I see a couple of swarthy RCMP recruits with fearless smiles and wholesome girlfriends of the secretarial persuasion. The guitarist cuts in on one of them, drifting off with the girl, keeping her at a respectful distance. The recruit suddenly looks very drunk, smiling stupidly at the two of them and snapping his fingers on the sideline.

Somehow, the last four decades of civilization have washed over The Arlington without disturbing a single hair on its head. You can hide in a time warp five or ten years prior to the beginning of rock and roll. Sweat up your suit. Find a woman just like dear old Mom.

The Balmoral

159 EAST HASTINGS STREET
PHONE: 681-8233
HOURS: MON–SAT: 11 A.M.–1 A.M.
SUN: 11 A.M.–MIDNIGHT

It's like New Year's Eve when people go purple trying to wring the last drops of fun from the calendar year. I'm pressed against the back wall away from all the drunken revelry. A friend beckoning from a table would be the passport to this party. I've got money for drinks and I'll punch the air to show the rock and roll spirit. Yikes! This is a pretty waitress. Beautiful down-sloping mouth and sturdy hips. A Native, too. My friend Ben says, "Guy, you're not really Canadian until you've had one." Then I memorized the names of the provinces for nothing.

A thin white-haired man propped up with a drinking glass full of cloudy white wine—clank glasses and smile. Take turns yelling into each other's ears. Sometimes when you get old, hair will start to flow out of your ears and there's not a damn thing you can do about it. When the band stops playing I ask him if he likes rock and roll. He says, "Yes, some of it is good," but I can tell he doesn't like it. There's a medallion around his neck claiming thirty days of sobriety. I roar with laughter, until I see the defeat blossoming in his eyes. He says, "Yeah, well, you know—actually, I just found this." He has opinions. These are his opinions:

> Bill Bennett didn't raise the welfare rates in four years. Old Man Bennett knew what he was doing. He could walk down the street, people would tip their hats. Bill, well, he'd get spit on and broken glass thrown in his face. Do you know why? I'll tell you why. Well Bill Bennett was too hard, too . . . you know, set in his ways. To be a good politician you have to be like a willow tree. You have to bend and roll like this, and Bill was no good at this . . . they talk about having no money. What a crock of shit. The war debt? Fuck. Let me tell you

something. Four hundred and fifteen billion dollars. Four hundred and fifteen billion fucken dollars. And I'll tell you something. Here's something. Take that war debt. They had it rated at thirty-two dollars an ounce of gold. They have six hundred, seven hundred million ounces of gold. At thirty-two dollars an ounce, don't forget that. Okay, take a base rate of, say, six or five, or say, fuck, say three hundred dollars an ounce, okay? Three hundred dollars an ounce. Gold mind you. At a base rate of three hundred dollars an ounce. Multiply that by the fucken amount of gold and the ounces, whatever, I mean you need a computer to do it—I've thought of doing it actually, anyway, guess what? There is no fucken war debt! Nothing! It's a crock of shit. They tell us that, so as long as the coffers are empty they can tax the Jesus out of us. Four hundred and fifteen billion dollars my ass. I'll tell you something about Vietnam. That's a situation happening to keep billionaires fat. Do you understand this? When they started pulling bullets out of American boys with "Made in America" on them [pointing to his temple] they started to figure it out. Sure. Fucken billionaires. Figure it out. And you know how the weapons came? Through France. Sure. France was neutral. France sold the weapons to Vietnam. Just like in World War Two. That's on their conscience. The government says they've got no money. What a crock of shit. The firecrackers at Expo? A hundred thousand dollars a night. They could afford to buy practically everyone on welfare a Cadillac with that kind of money. Here's something else. Do you know what's in fireworks? I'll tell you what. Potassium cyanide . . . well potassium . . . and sulphur. That's it! Sulphur. And they wonder why there's no fish in the lakes and they're spending *billions* cleaning it up. Hey, you know something? You're a good man. You're good to talk to. And you know something? You listen to me you'll learn.

Cairo's Pub

122 EAST HASTINGS STREET
PHONE: 684-9097
HOURS: 11 A.M. - 1 A.M.

One man stands alone on the dance floor shouting angrily at no one in particular. It sound like: "Chekhov! Chekhov! Chekhov, you assholes," but turns out to be: "Jerkmeoff!" and this sentiment is augmented with masturbatory gestures for the hearing impaired. He's making about as much impact as a small fart in the middle of a hurricane.

The band is climbing back onto the stage. I recognize the singer as the shaggy-haired kid who used to bag my groceries at the Safeway on West Tenth. He yanks the microphone from its stand and shouts into it, the ever-popular question: "DO YOU WANNA ROCK?" Not much reaction, so he has to ask us again and again until we're all screaming at him, and the kid is satiated. I feel as if I've just participated in an act of mass homosexuality.

The band is sponsoring a drinking contest. It's easy to enter. Just place a full glass of beer on the stage and when the singer says "Go!", you drink. I'm just getting the glass to my lips, thinking, *Christ I'm gunna win this*, when I hear a machine-gun burst of empty glasses hitting the stage, and then some muscular guy is holding the prize jug of beer above his head like it is the Stanley Cup. Empty glasses are thrust toward him as the band rips into Roll Over Beethoven and the migration to the dance floor begins.

I see a donkey-faced kid with greasy shoulder-length hair sitting quietly on the outskirts of a group of friends. When he gets up to buy himself a drink somebody takes his chair and so he stands patiently a few feet away sipping his drink. I'm thinking, *you poor donkey-faced kid*. When I turn around a few minutes later there is a beautiful girl perched on his lap.

The Dodson

25 East Hastings Street
PHONE: 681-6422
HOURS: MON–SAT: 9 A.M. –11 P.M; SUN: 11
A.M.–6 P.M.

The Dodson is the same size as my old high school gymnasium. The patrons move around as if they are recovering from major surgery. In heaven, one might expect to pop in here for a couple of cold beers, say, once a month; in hell, one would expect never to leave.

This old guy is earning a beer collecting empty glasses. When he stoops for a matchbox, I see thick hairs emerging from the crack of his elephantine buttocks. His nose looks like a sea cucumber. That'll start happening to me if I keep up this drinking. Put him on a poster with a beer in his hand and write STOP DRINKING! underneath. He turns to an elderly couple who are quietly nursing their beers, and says, "You owe me five dollars." The woman shakes her head without looking up. She says, "No, we paid you." There's lots of work downtown for a skilled mediator.

At the back of the bar there's a game of pool going on. A couple of hefty girls playing with a stylish old man. It's his shot. I could change a tire in the time it takes him to circle the table. Solar-powered drummer for sure. He isn't bothered by the woman raising her cue over his head and shouting: "Fucken do something!" He finally lowers himself over the ball. Shooting crisply, he redistributes the balls into fresh interesting patterns.

I sit around daydreaming. When I look up there is a large girl in front of me. After prolonged eye contact she informs me that I am "a fucken asshole" and "no big deal," confirming what I've always secretly suspected.

The Grand Union

74 WEST HASTINGS STREET
PHONE: 681-6611
HOURS: MON–SAT: 10 A.M.–MIDNIGHT; SUN:
11 A.M.–MIDNIGHT

More country and western music. I'm starting to understand it, and might soon fancy myself in a shirt with a bit of tassel dangling from the shoulders and sleeves. Give my enemies a good shitkicking instead of always hiring lawyers to harass them. I must be the youngest person in this bar.

I'm standing up here at the bar, just like Richard Gere in *Looking for Mr. Goodbar*. There's a sad-looking Native woman, and she says, "Would you like to join me and my sister for a drink?" She says, "I'll introduce you to my sister, she's pretty, and by the way, my name is Margaret, what's yours?"

We sink into an old couch where I can see the band and watch the Hastings Street turkey shoot through the open door. Margaret is from the Northwest Territories. She had seven brothers and sisters, two of them died. She asks, "Do you like me?" It's a lucky thing I do because I'm the worst liar in the world. There's her sister sitting with a table full of men. She has that odd style of glasses that look as if they are on upside down. It's nice here with Margaret. Her hand in my lap. I squeeze it and she says ouch. It is a hand with swollen purple knuckles and a U-shaped rip along one finger.

GUY: What happened here?
MARGARET: My old man bit me.
GUY: Get rid of him.
MARGARET: He's at home now. Pissed off too.
GUY: He's an animal to do that.
MARGARET: I deserve it.
GUY: Why?
MARGARET: I fuck around on him.
GUY: Well Margaret, that doesn't give him the right.
MARGARET: Fuck 'im.

30

199 EAST 21ST AVENUE

It's hard to come up with the correct facial expression while Margaret is french-kissing this man who snuck onto the couch with us. I'll try the one the dog owners use when they have to stop for doggie business. Hate to seem prudish and say, "Please take your hand out of my lap while you're doing that."

A few old couples shuffle around the dance floor; one woman staring down at her own body as if it might disappear. Margaret lifts her mangled fingers, and as I reach into my pockets for some change, fresh glasses of beer float down like snowflakes in front of my face.

Ivanhoe Hotel

1038 MAIN STREET
PHONE: 681-9118
HOURS: MON–SAT: 11 A.M.–1 A.M.

Here's an old guy drifting from table to table with his hands outstretched as if he's sleepwalking. I'd never think of massaging a stranger's head no matter how drunk I was. I see people laughing and pointing as soon as it's not happening to them.

It looks like a stage set in here with the brickwork peeking through the plaster in regular patterns. It's nice to be with people who don't shout at each other all the time.

I don't know how people can look so serious playing pool on these little tiny coin-operated pool tables. You'd think the game was a blueprint for the rest of their lives, and every miscalculation forecast a decade of frustration and failure. Look, I'll put my name on the chalkboard and show you how to fuck up with wild abandon.

A riveting document, this *Vancouver Sun*. I'm trying to understand the details of these latest Canucks trades. I don't blame the defenceman for wanting to be traded if he's booed every time he steps on the ice. It's hard enough showing up for work without ten thousand people booing you.

The world is full of surprises and I see that my old biochemistry teacher is beating everyone in the bar at pool. She's got a huge ass and a sinister smile. Biochemistry was my least favourite subject. When my name comes up, I rack the balls tight and grab the heaviest cue I can find. Never mind the crookedness so long as it weighs a ton. She's got a jackhammer break. Leaves me on the rail. Chalk up. I miss, and set her up for a run of stripes. Keep the look in my eye that suggests deep strategy. Just because you're sinking all your balls, it doesn't mean you're winning.

My shot. Chalk up. Shades of Paul Newman here for sure. Look at my balls: they're hovering over the pockets waiting to be banged in. Hurray! Down they go. A few heads turning now. She thought she had it wrapped up. Finally there is nothing but

1200 BLOCK GRANVILLE STREET

the eight ball between me and victory. It's a simple, direct, side pocket shot. Relax. Take my time. I want the ball to disappear from the table just as cleanly and unambiguously as all those biochemical pathways did from my memory. I shoot smoothly, and when I watch that eight ball roll quietly over the felt and bounce off the cushion, I know with certainty this is going to be the toughest decade of my life. I feel my face heating up as I watch her stoop down onto the ball. Yes that's right you fat bitch, put it in the corner because that side pocket needs repairing for sure.

The Ivanhoe is intimate and smug like Christmas time in a small college faculty lounge. The music is strictly Top 40, and there are no pretty women my own age. The Ivanhoe has no aspirations to trendiness or sexual perversity. It is a place where one may exist and drink in a most uncomplicated manner.

Metropole Hotel

320 ABBOTT STREET
PHONE: 682-6154
HOURS: MON–SAT: 10 A.M.–11 P.M;
SUN: 11 A.M.–7 P.M.

It's 3 o'clock in the afternoon. A fan turns slowly overhead, the walls are torn and grey. Everyone is drunk. I wouldn't stand a chance of catching up even if my liver was up to it. Some of the old guys live upstairs and they wander about in their house-coats growling and laughing at each other. It feels like a private club, or a Spanish ghetto, where shared history has stripped away the need for pretence.

There's an elderly woman in a red cotton dress sitting alone against the wall. She has a stylish white hat on, and a long string of pearls dangling from her neck. There is a tiny stage at the end of the bar where three old men (playing saxophone, piano and guitar) pour out a string of hits from the thirties and forties. The woman in the red dress throws out her arms and provides vocal accompaniment: a screeching drunken soprano, barely audible over the clatter and clanking of this beer-drenched afternoon. I look right into her eyes and suddenly she is looking into *my eyes*, singing *to me*. I'll have to try a variety of different smiles before I find the one expressing the correct degree of appreciation and embarrassment.

A hand falls softly on my shoulder. Look up and there's a man in a bowler hat looking down on me. "Are you boys from college?" he asks. My friend says, "No, we've been there. It's over. We work now." The old man introduces himself as Joe, with an Irish last name I cannot remember. I like him because even in his drunken state he understands the dynamics of a good conversation. And the way he rubs my shoulder I feel he's the coach, and I've pitched a good game.

> Look you boys, I'll tell you. Okay? I was a sign painter all my life. Made a good dollar. I can't complain. No, I had my share and I don't complain about it. But you college boys. Well, what the hell you guys. [to the

waitress] How would you like to dance with me? Put those beers down and dance with me you sweet thing. No? [back to us] I was a sign painter all my life and I can't complain about it. I had my fun. It's over now. Do you understand that? Over. I mean it's over. That's all right though. It's up to you now. I'm on old age pension now. Been on it for a long time. What the hell can I do about it now? We're in a depression. It took a war to get us out of the last one. Now listen here. You college boys. I hope to hell it doesn't take one to get us out of this. I was a sign painter. All my life. I could paint anything you wanted me to paint.

The waitress circulates with a tray of foamy beers. A patron says to her, "I saw you on *General Hospital* today," and she replies, "No you didn't, you asshole. *General Hospital* wasn't on today." A minute later she dashes out the front door shouting, "I'm leaving for a few minutes, you all behave yourself while I'm gone," and she nudges a man close to the door, warning him, "Don't fall asleep you!"

The woman in the red dress rises out of her chair and wobbles toward the dance floor. She pauses in the middle, jigging from one foot to the other. The men watch her, clapping their hands in time to the music. She bends both legs slightly and raises her dress high above her knees, displaying a remarkable set of legs and the dark outline of her pubic hair beneath a pair of translucent white stockings. Her dress falls and she strides triumphantly back to her seat, beginning to sing again.

Niagara Hotel

435 WEST PENDER STREET
PHONE: 688-7574
HOURS: MON–SAT: 11 A.M.–12 P.M; SUN: 11
A.M.–7:00 P.M.

Walking in out of the sun, I have to pause at the entrance and let my eyes adjust to the dim red glow. People are pushing behind me—sorry, go by me. Nobody in the seats against the walls, but farther in, a quiet gathering of sullen young men crowded around a spoon-shaped dance floor.

The lights fall down on a gorgeous brunette woman with broad shoulders and a big healthy mouth just like Carly Simon. She'd look great on a horse or under a waterfall or chasing children through a wheat field. She leans back on her knees rubbing oil into her genitals and mouthing the words to "Love is What You Make It." Evidently we have the Olympic Agony Team competing furiously along the sides of the stage.

Well Stan, I've been wrong in the past, but I think they look very, very good tonight. Even here in the preliminaries they seem to be in a great deal of agony. This team made a beautiful effort in Switzerland, and we're expecting a similar performance here. It's very exciting to watch as I'm sitting here, sweating in the booth. I don't see a flicker of hope or amusement in there anywhere. No, if they keep this up Stan, I think it's going to be extremely difficult to beat them, although we've been surprised by the Swedes in the past. Just a second! Something's happened. Oh my God! An unexpected turn here, late in the first round. A loss of concentration over there on the right, to the right of the dancer. The man in the faded jean jacket. He's clapping his hands together and pointing at the dancer, quite obviously enjoying himself. He's throwing his head back now, and he appears to be actually laughing. What a great shame. That will cost them the silver medal. The rest of

36

them are looking extremely agonized—a number of them signalling to the waitress for more drinks, but I'm afraid it won't be enough . . .

The second dancer is a thin girl with very long legs. She twirls around and around while ZZ Top's "Slip Inside My Sleeping Bag" pours out of the speakers. The DJ said her name is Jackie. Jackie is a good name for her. She has fine pouting face lips. I'd like to hear her talk about interesting things, like her childhood, her hatreds and her earliest memories. Catch myself leaning forward on the elbows like a chess pro. Watch out for my next move then.

You can't impress anyone at the Niagara. It's just a professionally run, unpretentious Canadian strip bar where you can get drunk for less than ten dollars.

Six Shooter Pub

1176 GRANVILLE STREET (REPLACED BY THE MAXIMUM BLUES PUB)

PHONE: 251-7932

HOURS: MON–SAT: NOON–MIDNIGHT.
SUN: 4 P.M.–10:30 P.M.

The conversion of the Old Blackstone into the Six Shooter, and the ensuing attempt at gentrification of clientele, raises serious questions about where one now goes to purchase weapons and low-grade heroin. Clicking his spurs and grinding his jaw most menacingly, the manager of The Six Shooter informed me that the riffraff have been driven out. Employing the age-old I'm-a-bit-of-a-dummy interviewing technique, I asked him exactly what kind of riffraff we were talking about. "Well," he said, "I just wouldn't care to describe them."

As the name suggests, the Six Shooter Pub is a country and western bar, featuring live music seven nights a week. All the staff wear cowboy boots and cowboy hats. Everyone keeps running to the centre of the room and extracting fistfuls of shelled peanuts from a wooden barrel. A policy of spitting the shells onto the floor has done away with the need for a carpet and has added to its saloon-like atmosphere.

I can't review the quality of the music because I don't understand country and western. I giggle when I hear a grown man sing about the quality of his hangover, and how pissed off he is at the little woman who ran away with a trucker, taking all the furniture with her. There's a set of cultural sensibilities there that I simply don't possess.

There was a crowd of people whooping and hollering on the dance floor. They transferred their weight from one foot to the other, occasionally falling down from the exertion.

The Sunrise Hotel

101 EAST HASTINGS

PHONE: 685-8719

HOURS: MON–SAT: 9 A.M.–11 P.M;

SUN: 11 A.M.–11 P.M.

Once as a teenager I witnessed an ugly fight in front of the Sunrise during which one man attacked another with a broken beer bottle. Being an impressionable little guy from an essentially nonviolent background, I became afraid of the place. When I was living downtown at the age of nineteen, the Sunrise was probably the only bar in town I had not drunk at.

Having my first beer in the Sunrise was a bit like losing my virginity; although I wasn't relaxed enough to enjoy myself, it was easily bearable and I gave myself a mental karate chop for not jumping in there sooner. The police strolled around checking ID, thrusting their fingers down inside the socks of patrons and shining light onto their pubic hair.

A young woman waddles in. She isn't much higher than the handles of my bicycle. She scans the bar before sitting down at my table; the fat of her thighs flattening out against the plastic seat cover and the greasy brown hair falling away from her face to reveal a pasty smile and the flesh above her eyebrows raw from all the plucking. She says, "Why don't you buy me a beer?" I say, "I'm just leaving." She says, "Hey it won't kill you."

This is her story. Two weeks ago she was living in Toronto with her husband and child. The husband beats the hell out of her. He never works. He keeps promising not to beat the hell out of her any more and she keeps forgiving him. It never works. Well, she was sitting around with her mother, real drunk and depressed, and it dawned on her that she probably needed a holiday. Her mother lent her $500 for a plane ticket to Vancouver and agreed to take care of the child. She didn't want to sober up in case she lost her nerve and got stuck in Toronto forever. In Vancouver she went straight to welfare and picked up a cheque and got even drunker. She has a room at the Balmoral for $75 a week. It's okay, but Vancouver really sucks and she can't wait

39

27 EAST PENDER STREET

---

to leave. As soon as the next cheque comes in, it's bye-bye and back to Toronto. But never back to that husband unless he changes.

Princeton Hotel

1901 POWELL STREET

PHONE: 253-6020

HOURS: MON–SAT: 9:30 A.M.–11:30 P.M;

SUN: 11 A.M.–11 P.M.

It's a drizzly Vancouver morning. Plodding along the railway tracks out of Gastown, straight toward the prairies. I must buy a trench coat and learn to do Bogart. There's the sugar refinery on my left, and B.C. Marine where I was a welder before the recession. If I step on the gravel between these slabs of wood I'll disappear into the earth forever.

Swing through these doors and land in the lap of a comfortable leather chair. Sometimes the Princeton Hotel is the logical midpoint between Gastown and the prairies. Draught beer is the thing. Never drink it with quiche or say the word "lovely" between sips.

There is an elderly man with long silver hair reading a western in one corner. I'm not usually up at this time in the morning. A white kid and an Indian kid sitting opposite each other. The white kid is lifting his glass in the air, raising his voice. He is willing to bet $50 that you can stuff a V-8 into a Datsun. There's a group of tidy middle-aged men perched on stools at the bar. They are laughing and slapping each other on the back as if they're golfers, playing well for the first time in years. Through the walls of the bar, a solitary seagull crying in the distance. These could well be the most civilized alcoholics sitting in the most civilized bar in town.

I ask to talk to the manager but instead I get the owner. I can tell right away that he is a man who knows right from wrong: clean cut in a cowboyish sort of way, and a strong lingering handshake. His name is Mike Kahut. He starts a model train moving around the walls of the bar above my head. It whistles and the front engine throws up a tiny puff of smoke. Mike Kahut looks very proud. At night his son comes in to manage the bar for him. He's owned The Princeton for thirty-five years. This was a month or so before Expo 86 was set to open.

41

COMMERCIAL AND KITCHENER

GUY: Do you think you'll catch the Expo business out here?
MR KAHUT: [looking slightly guilty] Jeez, I kinda hope not.

The train disappears into a tunnel. The walls are lined with photographs of old steamships and trains. I'll try nursing this beer instead of always guzzling. Feel the warmth of this bar. Like an ordinary evening in the middle of an extended family.

The Waldorf Cocktail Lounge

1489 EAST HASTINGS STREET
PHONE: 253-7141
HOURS: MON–SUN: 11 A.M.–1 A.M.

There are some things about cocktail waitresses that you can depend on: they have pretty names, they shave their armpits, they want to travel, they love animals and they have tidy apartments with cablevision. Of course all those things are true of me too.

The Waldorf Cocktail Lounge was built in 1955. It's a replica of a Hawaiian bar. The best way to imagine it is to picture the Planetarium dropped into the middle of a jungle and left there to mature. A galaxy of sparkling pin lights set into a deep blue ceiling gives the effect of permanent twilight. The bamboo counter snakes across the room, framed by palm trees and Hawaiian art. There's a colour television set above the bar. All is dark and quiet and cool. You could fall in love with your enemies sitting around this place.

The cocktail waitress brings me a beer. She has luscious pale lips and cascading blonde hair. Her name is Trisha, and she sits beside me on a stool, bravely pre-empting World Cup Soccer in favour of *The Newlywed Game*. She is smiling, swirling the ice around in her drink. That's a sound for sore ears. With a bit of luck I'll have a wife like Trisha, and we'll vacation in Hawaii while my three goofy playboy sons tend the sprawling network of steel mills back home.

The four new brides have purple faces. They sit alone in their booths, completing the sentence: "It really makes my husband's blood boil when I call him _____." They said Genit, Tibro, Sugar and Stupid. When the husbands came back they guessed Genit and Tibro but not Sugar and Stupid. There was laughter, hugging, frowning and slapping in all the logical places.

The West Hotel

444 CARRALL STREET
PHONE: 681-8374
HOURS: MON–SUN: 11 A.M.–1 A.M.

After my first lesson I ask my piano teacher if she will come and have a drink with me. Closing the lid of the piano carefully with her long soft hands, she says, "It's rather irregular." I say, "Yes I agree, it's rather irregular."

Twenty minutes later, splashed red and blue from a strobing police car, we weave our way past the mumbling masses and in through the doors of the West Hotel. We are the only customers. She says, "Hmmm, well let's sit down here." It's the brightest table in the house, and I don't like it, but I sit and order eight beers. Her eyebrows go up as if I am a small boy not to be trusted with kitchen appliances.

In the washroom I deposit a quarter into a slot machine advertising itself as *A Chest Full of Zany and Funny Novelties.* There's a promising clunk from within the machine and down below I receive a cardboard package containing a plastic coin. On one side of the coin it says: Big cats are very dangerous, and on the other side it says: But a little pussy won't hurt anyone. As I dry my hands under the flow of warm air, a fat bearded Frenchman shuts himself in one of the stalls, advising me that he is about to take a huge shit.

My piano teacher is not one to mince words. She plainly does not like the West Hotel. While I was gone some thoughtless swine stole one of my beers and called her a cunt. She removes her coat from the back of her chair and leaves before I can answer the question she asks me: *what kind of a man are you?*

Hair

Once there was a small boy called Alex, living in Cambridge, England, with his mother, father and sister. His father was an unsuccessful stockbroker. Mick Jagger lived a few hundred miles away, a virgin, weight-lifting diligently in his back yard.

Every Sunday, the family gathered together some stale bread and they rode their bicycles to the mossy banks of the Cam where they fed the trumpeter swans and watched the Cambridge University rowing team, training in synchronized agony.

On his way to school Alex was routinely waylaid by two sisters who would pinch his cheeks until he cried. At school he was lively and arrogant. Not everyone liked him. One day he got in a fight with a tough, ginger-haired kid named Marvin. To his surprise, he was able to pin Marvin's shoulders to the ground with his knees.

Grabbing a fist full of hair he smashed the back of Marvin's head into the concrete, causing it to bleed. Alex immediately felt that he had used too much force. So did the headmaster who happened to be looking our his window at the time. Alex learned the art of apologizing under pressure.

When he was nine years old the whole family moved to New York State. They sailed across the Atlantic on a luxury ocean liner called *The France*. It was the longest ocean liner in the world. It took half an hour just to walk around it. Alex and his sister both had their own rooms. They learned to play ping pong.

One evening Alex was sitting on the deck of the swimming pool waiting for his food to digest when he noticed a middle-aged couple staring at him. They seemed to be having an argument about him. He felt very uncomfortable and started to wish that he was invisible. The woman walked over to him. Her skin was brown and wrinkled. She had a horrible smile, worse than a salesman's because it wasn't practised. She said, "Tell me, my husband and I are having an argument. Are you a boy or a girl?"

Ho Wah Men's Hairstylist

123 EAST HASTINGS STREET
PHONE: 688-5751
HOURS: MON–SAT: 9 A.M.–5 P.M.
ADULT CUT: $6.50

There's not much in the way of small conversation here. Two Chinese guys are ahead of me but they're almost bald. One of them smells like brake fluid. He's wearing a lime green cardigan. I must be the only white man ever to come in here. Feel a bit awkward. Unfold the newspaper and remember to move my head up and down to show that I am reading it. My Chinese is rusty, but I see the word "transmission" in there for sure.

Sun pouring in through the glass onto the back of my neck. Lots of guys running around outside with styrofoam cups of coffee. White circular speakers embedded in the ceiling. I heard this same arrangement of "Helter Skelter" in the Safeway the other week. Don't know if John Lennon would have approved. I sort of miss the guitar parts.

I don't have to wait long. When my turn comes I step up into the chair and see my face all pale and pimply in the mirror. It's impossible to relax with this white robe draped over my body. Smile at Mr. Chow and he gives one back. He says he's cut hair in this room for twenty years and before that in Hong Kong. I'll ask Mr. Chow all about Hong Kong, because I'm broke and this is how I do my travelling.

GUY: What is Hong Kong like, Mr. Chow?
MR. CHOW: Yes.
GUY: No. [slowly] What is Hong Kong like? Is it a nice place?
MR. CHOW: Waa?
GUY: I'm interested in Hong Kong. Hong Kong.
MR. CHOW: Hong Kong?
GUY: Right.
MR. CHOW: Hong Kong [shaking his head] . . . lossa people.

4601 MAIN STREET

I know English is a tricky language, but I think after twenty years one might hope for a higher level of proficiency. The hair cut took exactly six minutes. I told him, "A little off the top and the sides," but from the look of things I might as well have said, "I'm joining the marines. Go for it!" Despite this, Mr. Chow's pleasant chairside manner and his spectacularly succinct population analysis of Hong Kong left me feeling that it was $6.00 well spent.

Unfortunately, the reaction to Mr. Chow's work was, on the whole, negative. "Whoa there, Squarehead!," "Oh well, it'll grow back," and "Ha, ha, ha!" were among the rude and hurtful things said to me in the twenty-four hours following my trip to Ho Wah's. I have a hunch that Mr. Chow is simply too far ahead of current trends to gain acceptance in the plebian ranks.

Capital
Barber Shop

60 East Hastings Street
PHONE: 669-9438
HOURS: MON—SAT: 8 A.M.–6:00 P.M.
ADULT CUT: $5.00

This old man sitting across from me looks like Judge Roy Bean. Lots of frizzy white hair, wide brown suspenders, and a set of false teeth floating around inside his head. When I smile at him he bats his eyelids, which is a pretty strange thing for an old man to do.

Mr. Lui throws the white cape over me and then he pulls $2.00 out of the cash register and hands it to the old man. The old man looks up and waves the money away. He says, "No, I tricked you. I want a shave too." It's an embarrassing moment, with Mr. Lui silently shoving the $2.00 back in the till and the old guy laughing so hard his teeth pop out.

I tell Mr. Lui, "Just a trim today," and let's hope he heard me because I'll sue if I get teased after this one. I know from the way he pushes my head around with the body of the scissors that Mr. Lui made the right decision not going into medicine. He sprays the side of my head with water. The cool mist feels odd inside my ear. This is the last place in the world I expect to be aroused, but then you read about guys doing it with sheep, and women with donkeys in Mexico.

I'm becoming the world's most versatile small conversationalist. It turns out that Mr. Lui is from South China. I ask him about some of the differences between living in South China and British Columbia. If Mr. Lui were strong, he would be the strong silent type. Never a guy to pontificate endlessly, he taps my head with his scissors and produces this patriotic summation: "better here." On the subject of Chinese restaurants, he says they are all they same and he doesn't bother going because his wife will cook him the same stuff at home for a fraction of the cost. Mr. Lui, you've certainly found the good life we are all searching for.

49

195 EAST 26TH AVENUE

I received no qualitative references to my Capital hair cut, which could be a good sign. However, given that the B.C. economy is in utter shambles, and Mr. Lui is obviously not going to recirculate a dime of your $5.00, I suggest you go elsewhere.

Guido's

44 EAST HASTINGS STREET

PHONE: NONE

HOURS: 8 A.M.–5 P.M. (EXCEPT WEDNESDAYS)

ADULT CUT: $8.00

Despite the staggering $8.00 fee, I decided to give Guido's a shot. I think a man with a name like Guido usually knows what he is doing.

I plod through the rain only to find that Guido is not there. There is a tidy white man in a blue sweater reading a newspaper. He's old enough to have small grandchildren. He offers to shine my shoes. I say, "Where's Guido?" He says, "Guido hasn't worked a Wednesday in over thirty years!" I challenge him to turn my grey boots black. He says, "I can do that, but I don't know how long they'll stay that way."

The Shoeshine Man says, "You're the only customer I've had today," and he starts to paint my boots with black dye. A very sick looking man in a purple jacket presses his face hard against the window. He looks around the shop and bursts out laughing. The Shoeshine Man says, "People say they have rights too, but a lot of them would be better off in institutions. They sleep in doorways and under bridges. Some of them can't even panhandle. What good is that?"

A whale of a man comes wheezing through the doorway, fussing that his parking meter is about to expire and he can't find a decent umbrella. The Shoeshine Man says, "If he comes back, do you mind if I do him while the dye soaks into your boots?" I don't mind. I don't know why I am so content on this miserably rainy day. There's nothing in my head, nothing in my heart.

The Whale comes back. He has to clutch the side of the shoeshine stand to hoist himself up there. He says, "Hey, do you know where I can get a good umbrella? I'm looking for a really good one, so that if I swing it at a dog it will break the dog's head open." Then to the Shoeshine Man, he says, "I think you shined my shoes before." But the Shoeshine Man cannot remember him.

WHALE: Hey, you're doing manual labour but you're not sweating.

SHOESHINE MAN: That's bad.

WHALE: No, it's good. It means you're in shape.

SHOESHINE MAN: I know, but I'm not in shape.

WHALE: Well, you're not sweating.

SHOESHINE MAN: I know . . . but the thing is, I'm not in shape.

There's a discussion which culminates in the three of us agreeing that when you drive, it's hard not to scuff up the heel of the right shoe. I don't know how long we sit around agreeing on that fact.

The Shoeshine Man shows me a collection of antique metal printing plates. He holds them up to the mirror one by one so that we can read them. I tell him exactly what he wants to hear—that they are special, valuable things. Walk away past the fallen bodies and desperate ragged ghosts who hack their lungs out onto the concrete. Never had such shiny boots before. Feel quite indestructible as I hop and skip along the way.

Central Barbers

309 CAMBIE STREET
PHONE: NONE
HOURS: MON–SAT: 9 A.M.–4:30 A.M.
ADULT CUT: $5.00

My hair is so short by now that I don't see how this guy will find anything to cut. If I see even a hint of ridicule on his face, I'll say, "Look, I'm in the army and it's not allowed to touch my ears." Just my luck, one of these old guys lining the wall will perk up and ask me what division I'm in. I'll have to say, "I don't know what division I'm in. I'm a pathological liar, okay?" That's one for emergencies only; it's clumsy and ugly, but it gets them off your back.

Here comes a paunchy old man, hunched over into the first snow of the year, wheezing along the sidewalk with a wooden cane. He is bald on top but there's a ring of thick brown hair coming out the sides. He comes in chuckling to himself. He says "Whew, I'm out of breath . . . saw a friend of mine down there by Woodward's. I tried to catch him, but I couldn't. He disappeared. I lost him." After he catches his breath he lifts the end of his cane up so that it is pointing out the window across the street. He says, "You know, that beer parlour across the street is doing business. Christ. Seventy-five cents a glass. I can never understand that. Guys sitting in beer parlours. I never sat in a beer parlour in all my life. A guy took me into one a long time back and it was boring. They can shove it up their asses."

This place is warm and there's a poster of a topless woman with huge flat nipples and silky, shoulder-length black hair. She looks strong and sophisticated, with none of the sluttish features I've come to expect from barber shop pin-ups. Five guys waiting for a haircut. I'll just sit here and listen to the sound of the conversational ball bouncing.

It's two days before the Vancouver mayoral election. I tell the group of elderly men that I don't think Harry Rankin will be our next mayor. The paunch man looks at me with wide challenging eyes. He says, "Why not?" I say, "Well, I'm pretty left-wing I

53

think, and I'm not going to vote for him." Some chord has been plucked here; the man, redistributing himself all over the seat, running the cane up and down between his fingers. This is the first real political conversation of my life. He says. "Why not?" I know I can sabotage my point by getting too excited, so I speak in the most casual manner, as if the topic is one on which I am the undisputed world expert but my interests lie elsewhere. I say, "You know, Harry Rankin is a lawyer and he was trained on the adversary system. He thinks that to win territory, he has to go out and knock the other man down. Now, that's absolutely true in law, but I don't think politics works that way. I think the way the system is set up, a man who knows how to win friends will be a better mayor for Vancouver." For sure I've overdone it. This guy has metamorphosed into a vibrating beetroot. He points his cane in my face and says, "You've got a lot to learn, my boy. Jesus Christ you've got a lot to learn. You vote for the ideology, not the man. Always, the ideology." He looks past me, out the window of the barber shop, mumbling to himself, "You know, I worry about you youngsters. There's no hope really. I mean, honestly now, Jesus Christ, I just don't know what to say to you."

Those electric clippers feel great on my neck, and the hum of them mesmerizes me. A conversation seeps in though my ears and chews up a bite of memory.

PAUNCH MAN: Hey, is your mother still alive?

BARBER: No, no. She passed away two years ago.

PAUNCH MAN: Right, right. Hey, I didn't know your brother had two heart attacks.

BARBER: No?

PAUNCH MAN: No.

BARBER: Well, he did.

PAUNCH MAN: Yeah, I ran into him a while back. He told me he'd had two heart attacks.

BARBER: That was ten years ago.

PAUNCH MAN: Both of them, ten years ago?

BARBER: Yeah.

PAUNCH MAN: Well, that's pretty good.

BARBER: Oh yeah. That's real good.

PAUNCH MAN: Sure, I mean ten years ago . . .

BARBER: Say, you remember Ida?

PAUNCH MAN: That fucken bitch!

BARBER: No kidding?

PAUNCH MAN: The one married that Scotsman?

BARBER: I don't know.

PAUNCH MAN: Worked in a bakery?

BARBER: Yeah!

PAUNCH MAN: Well, she's quite a conceited bitch from way back.

BARBER: She'd be about seventy-two now.

PAUNCH MAN: That's right.

BARBER: Did she have kids?

PAUNCH MAN: A son. He was a teacher.

BARBER: Is that right?

PAUNCH MAN: He got the shit kicked out of him.

BARBER: No kidding?

PAUNCH MAN:He was a fucken stool pigeon.

BARBER: No kidding?

PAUNCH MAN: He got the shit kicked out of him.

BARBER: Is that right?

PAUNCH MAN: The guy was a fucken stool pigeon.

Of course it was only a trim, and I haven't seen the back of it yet, but I think my hair looks great. I'll be back at Central Barbers, and next time I'll be talking religion.

251 EAST HASTINGS STREET

Skin

The Drake

606 POWELL STREET
PHONE: 254-2826
HOURS: MON–SAT: 11 A.M.–1 A.M; SUN: 11
A.M.–MIDNIGHT

The Drake has made the dubious decision to go upscale while preserving the tradition of continuous dancing girls. Now, while sitting in a room full of drunk men, watching beautiful women you are never going to touch, you may contemplate not only that you are doing this, but that you have dressed up to do it.

The clientele are almost exclusively male, and mostly Oriental. The dancers have several things in common:

1) femaleness
2) fashion model smiles
3) very short pubic hair
4) sexual confidence

The Drake understands a bit about human psychology. This is what I figure they figure: like little kids, we are drawn to what we cannot have. These dancers are cookies on the top shelf of life, so high up that most of us will never be able to reach them. But, if someone wants to take the cookies down, display them and put them back, people will sit quietly and watch it. This ritual of temptation and deprivation, repeated over and over, breeds misery. The Drake has an antidote for misery. They sell it by the glass. I've never used the star system to rate a club. Now I see the power of it. I'll scale mine like this:

*   poor
**   mediocre
***   better than average
****   made me proud to be human

—and I'll give The Drake only one star (*) because it made me

4323 MAIN STREET

---

horny and depressed, it cost too much to get drunk, and the waiters looked silly in their little red waistcoats.

The New Penthouse

1019 SEYMOUR STREET
PHONE: 683-2111
HOURS: MON–SAT: 8 P.M.–2 A.M.

In an era when exotic dancing has become intensely gynecological, the "no spreading" policy of the Penthouse shifts you mercifully back into the arena of the sensual. It's lunchtime in the upstairs lounge. I'll slip in here beside an older couple who smile at me and lift their drinks. They're friendly, just like Americans on a train. A sprinkling of young men in dark suits sit rigidly in their seats as if they are awaiting further orders. A black woman lies naked on her stomach at my feet. Rolling over, she waves politely at a man who is leaving and he blows her a kiss. She slithers over the floor and the look in her eye is a jolt because there is more warmth than sex there. I'm trying to stop looking so I can write something.

Later, wrapped in a black satin housecoat, the dancer sits down beside me.

> DANCER: [pointing to the pen and paper] Okay, what's the official business here?
> GUY: I'm trying to write a small book.
> DANCER: Oh.
> GUY: Do you dance here full time?
> DANCER: No. I dance all over town.
> GUY: It's quiet here. Do you miss the roar of the crowds?
> DANCER: [something maternal and instructing in her tone] I get paid the same whether the crowds roar or not.

Later in the day I'm on the phone making an appointment to meet Ross Filippone, the owner of the New Penthouse. I show up in a jacket and tie, a notebook and pen in hand. Ross Filippone is a big man: tanned, bespectacled, suited. His handshake means business, but it's not one of those bone-crunchers that makes you wonder what's going on inside the guy's head. It's just a firm handshake without a hint of femininity or the recession in it. Develop one of those myself and I'll be a car owner before long for sure.

The following conversation has been reconstructed from memory. I have a good memory for conversations so I think it is accurate.

ROSS FILIPPONE: The Penthouse is the oldest night club in Vancouver. There were four Filippone brothers. Two of them have passed away. It started as a bottle club back in the forties; a place where you'd come with a group of friends and bring a bottle of whiskey with you. You'd buy a bowl of ice for a quarter and a few bottles of Coke and you were set for the evening.

GUY: Was that legal?

ROSS FILIPPONE: Well, no it wasn't, but the police turned a blind eye to it. It was understood. You see, back in those days the Hotel Association controlled the liquor business. They didn't want anyone else to sell liquor so we had to sneak around like that.

GUY: Did you have strippers back then?

ROSS FILIPPONE: No, no, no . . . nothing like that. Just live bands. Popular bands playing what were then the hits of the day. Then along came a thing called the Vancouver Cabaret Association. There were about thirty clubs involved. We lobbied against the liquor laws, which were very archaic. Embarrassing really. People would visit and see policemen running around like Keystone Cops, looking under the tables for booze. If they found a bottle you'd just say: "Whoa, how the hell did that get there?" Much simpler than paying the fine. Finally in the late forties it came to a plebiscite. People voted in favour of the new booze laws. The Cave and the Palomar were the first two clubs in town to receive cabaret licences. They brought in big-name acts like Louis Armstrong and Duke Ellington. For some reason, political or whatever, the Penthouse was the very last club to receive a cabaret licence. We were the last bottle club in town.

GUY: And then the girls?

ROSS FILIPPONE: Yes.

GUY: Local girls?

ROSS FILIPPONE: No, there were no local strippers at that time. We brought them in from L.A., Chicago, New York. Just topless, mind you. I was never in favour of bottomless dancers. As all the bars started hiring girls it got more and more explicit. Finally, we were the only club in town that wouldn't allow the girls to take off their bottoms. I started getting complaints. More complaints than compliments. I had to change. But I still won't allow them to spread. Who wants to see that?

GUY: It's degrading.

ROSS FILIPPONE: Well, yes, but they hire those really young girls and people pay to watch them spread. I can't go for it. I mean, I've got a wife and kids. I couldn't take my wife out to see stuff like that. I try to book acts with a little class. This week we've got Miss Hungary. Hell of a nice girl. No hanky panky or anything like that. Her husband, that is, her manager, brought her over here. He didn't want me to use the title Miss Hungary because of the pavilion at Expo, and I understand that it could be an embarrassment for the family or the country or whatever, but for the kind of money I'm paying for her, I don't have any choice. She's not really a dancer. Her husband persuaded her to do it I guess. So here she is: Miss Hungary. Very sweet girl. Very good manners.

GUY: I'd like to see her.

ROSS FILIPPONE: [refering to his watch] She's on in half an hour.

GUY: I'll stick around.

ROSS FILIPPONE: Sure, it's a clean act.

GUY: Before I go there's something I'd like to ask you. It might make you angry. The word on the street is that you are connected with the Mafia. Could you respond?

ROSS FILIPPONE: When you have been in the trucking business and you are from Italian descent, people have a tendency to talk. It doesn't bother me. It's just talk. If you want to mention places like Chicago and Montreal, then yes, I

1000 BLOCK GRANVILLE

know for a fact that organized crime exists there. Drugs, prostitution, gambling, things like that. I have three children of my own. Here are their pictures. Thank God none of them do drugs. I've never so much as taken a puff of marijuana. Who needs it? If I want to get high then I can go and have a couple of drinks. That's if I want to get high mind you.

Miss Hungary is a pretty one, pacing the stage like a wooden panther. When she stretches her arms up over her head I can see two or three ribs poking through underneath her breasts. Smile at her and she waves just like the Queen of England. When I wave back I think everyone can figure out we know each other. And this drink courtesy of Mr. Filippone. Oh boy! I want to be the kind of person who knows a lot of people. Some of them with titles like Sultan, Chancellor, Miss, and so forth. Hanging over the bar, there's a coin the size of a baby elephant. The head of a Greek King crying his eyes out.

Kitty Kat Theatre

MAIN & 7TH

10 A.M. - 2:00 A.M.

$6 SINGLE; $4 SENIOR; $9 COUPLE

Contrary to popular belief, most pornographic films boast strong plots, skilled actors and innovative direction. Although production values are unlikely to meet the standards of *Batman* or *Black Robe*, these forty-minute allegorical films routinely tackle themes of self-discovery and national unity—and, unlike the sanitized assembly-line product filing out of Tinseltown, films like *Gang Bang Betty* and *Hot Cocks From Hell* offer the viewer a complex, ambiguous, challenging vision of spirituality and human nature.

The Kitty Kat Theatre has a small lobby with a private phone and a few comfortable plastic chairs. I purchase my ticket from an elderly turbaned man. A blatantly unconstitutional notice taped to the glass counter advises: "No Refund for Seniors."

Eight dim bulbs line the concrete walls of the 120-seat theatre, casting a faint glow across the backs of the dozen men who sit there. I choose a seat way off to one side for discreet note-taking. With my luck they'll spot my hand moving and just like Pee Wee Herman I'll be cut off from the neighbourhood children. Lose the most precious part of my day, when they crowd around, call me Guy Smiley and beg for helicopter rides. No good saying it was research, either. Better to hold the head high and hint at past abuses.

In the first film, *Sex Star,* a young porno star is dismissed from the film set because she freezes during girl-girl scenes. She works off her frustration playing squash with a shaggy-haired acquaintance whose nostrils are compressed into thin slits. After squash the women make love separated from each other by a translucent sliding glass door. When they finally open the door, it turns out they both have abnormally long tongues with some localized spasticity there.

Through her squash partner, Thirsty is introduced to two men, one of whom looks like a spider. They go on a double date.

1000 BLOCK GRANVILLE SOUTH SIDE

After dinner the foursome tear off each other's clothes, sucking and probing like newborn sparrows. I had wrongly assumed the spidery guy, played by Jack Mehoff, would turn out to have an incongruously large penis. In fact it is carrot-like, full of indentations and eccentric rings, tapering pathetically at the end. His torso is white and hairless and devoid of muscle tone, while his atrophied legs are smothered with a mat of black hair. Despite his repulsiveness and the general coarseness of the company, he is allowed to suck and probe right along with the more attractive people.

After the second feature I am followed to the washroom by a dark, acne-scarred man in a waist-cut leather jacket. He pushes himself into the urinal beside me, his hip firmly against mine. Immediately, every sphincter in my urinary system slams shut.

As I bolt past the group of Sikhs chatting in the lobby and out onto the street, I glance over my shoulder to see the man hovering in the doorway of the washroom—a soft, ingratiating smile playing across his pock-marked face.

Kitten Theatre

1026 GRANVILLE STREET
10 A.M. TO MIDNIGHT
$6 SINGLE, $4 SENIORS

It's so dark I won't sit down for fear of being impaled on a stranger's lap. The first feature, *Cat Woman*, deals with a young woman's struggle for identity and self-respect after the dissolution of her marriage. Our vulnerable heroine meets an unemployed man who informs her that she is a cat. "I'm *not* a cat," she protests. Moments later they have anal sex, and she mysteriously capitulates: "I guess I *am* a cat."

Next she is thrown into a small room full of autistic women caked with make-up.

> SHE: I thought I was Queen of the pride.
> HE: I want you to prove yourself.
> SHE: By fighting them?
> HE: No, you must win them with caresses.

The second feature, *Confessions of a Middle-Aged Nympho*, explores dialectical materialism and the phenomenon of promiscuity among the aging. Sandwiched between two bouts of conventional sex with her husband (a simple-minded white-collar worker), the Middle-Aged Nympho is penetrated inventively by a multi-national task force of have-nots. The socio-economic trajectory of the American Negro is brilliantly charted in a scene where a pot-bellied black actor waves his flaccid penis in the face of the Middle-Aged Nympho, ordering her sharply to "Suck my meat"—a clear reference to Jesse Jackson's failed Democratic presidential nomination bid.

During a scene of quadruple penetration, the patron in the seat directly behind me begins masturbating noisily. At first I attempt to dismiss the wet slapping sound as an auditory hallucination, but eventually I am convinced by the crescendoing vibrations transferred through his knees to the back of my seat. Cowering miserably, I brace for an onslaught of leaping grey fluids.

GEORGIA VIADUCT, MIDNIGHT

Finally, when it seems clear the man is on the verge of a biochemical catharsis, my inertia is overwhelmed by revulsion and common sense. I dart to the front of the theatre and flop next to a dowdy young couple who greet my arrival with conspiratorial whispers. Propping my legs on an inverted plastic bucket, I attempt to re-engage myself with the plight of the Middle-Aged Nympho.

I don't recommend the Kitten for first-time porn theatregoers. It's very dark and can be extremely intimidating. There is a magazine section and a line of sex toys in the lobby. The inflatable doll seems on the verge of an important utterance. The bumpf on the package promises: "You will never be bored or lonely again."

Haida Theatre

3215 KINGSWAY
11:00 A.M. TO 11:30 P.M.
$6.00 SINGLE, $10.50 COUPLES
PH. 435-2333

Directly opposite Carlton Elementary School, a ten-foot length of red carpet projects from the doorway of the Haida onto the sidewalk. To gain access to the Couples Only balcony, I reluctantly enlist the services of my wife Lora (having mentally rejected every other female I know—starting with my mother and ending with my parole officer). We purchase two root beers and a hot dog at the concession stand and head up to the cool balcony where there's ample leg room, bench seats and wall-to-wall indoor-outdoor carpeting.

The first feature, *Hometown Honeys*, involves a sexual contest between two working class bisexual women. Malnourished and sorely in need of orthodontic work, they take turns inserting each other anally with an arundinaceous dildo. There is something almost medically brusque about their methodology.

A wiry man charges up the steps past us into the projection room as we jump to the bedroom of an Asian couple who are videotaping themselves making love. The woman has an impossibly thin voice, like the death cry of a field mouse inflated with helium, and her husband is a game sort who repeatedly jabs his tongue into her hairless rectum.

By this time I am beginning to regret having brought my wife. Pale and stoic under the flickering light, she's accustomed to men with unionized jobs. I'm summoning an apology, an explanation, a disclaimer of sorts, when suddenly she belts out, "Now there's a really decent-sized cock!"

The Haida is Vancouver's most relaxing adult theatre. There's an intimate lobby where you can sit around obscured from pedestrians by panels of smoked glass. My friend Jeff Keller says these films are just to help men masturbate, but I sense something else here too.

Message to owner: Your cashier is skimming the till. My wife

VALUE VILLAGE, 1820 EAST HASTINGS STREET

and I were rerouted *around* the turnstile, scrutinized under the pretext that we appeared to be teenagers. This is hardly plausible. I am thirty-three. My wife has just cracked thirty. After three years of living with me she looks seven years older than I do. (It doesn't seem to matter how young I marry them, they end up overtaking me—a bully's karma.)

XXX Adult Super Store

58 E. HASTINGS

A muscular, fleshy-lipped young man ushers me toward a display of pornographic magazines, videos, and sexual paraphernalia. Immediately catching my eye are *The Expanding Butt Plug, The Striker Penis Pump,* and a family-size box of *Hospital Examination Gloves.* Wilting with embarrassment, I have to remind myself: I'm only shopping here—this guy *works* here, or maybe *owns* the place.

As I browse through the Gay Magazines section, a portly, dishevelled man enters and abruptly launches into a monologue about the sexual habits of East Indians. He claims that "over there," mothers make love to their sons, fathers deflower their daughters—and, furthermore, the police pay them to do it. The proprietor shakes his head in amazement as though we are all blessed to have this fountain of knowledge in our midst. As the monologue winds down, the man steps forward and buys a package of flavoured condoms.

PORTLY MAN: See ya.
PROPRIETOR: You bet. Going roller skating today?
PORTLY MAN: Nah, too many people in Stanley Park.
PROPRIETOR: Fuck it eh?
PORTLY MAN: Yeah, plus I got an interview with a computer
    company.

I purchase a fistful of tokens and climb into one of the cramped booths in the back room. There is a padded bench seat for my bum, a plastic circulation grid above my head, a flimsy deadbolt to keep the plywood door shut. A 14-inch colour television set says, WELCOME TO THE ADULT SUPERSTORE #2, offering me a choice of eight channels with programs like *TV*

4102 MAIN STREET

Fuck Party, Fuck My Mouth, and *Angelo Loves It.* Despite the fact that the booth is supplied with a roll of toilet paper and a waste bin, things are very slippery underfoot.

I deposit my tokens and channel-hop through a kaleidoscope of unconventional penetrations. Angelo is endowed with male genitalia and a modest pair of breasts dotted with jet-black nipples. On another channel, a buck-toothed strumpet receives a penis up her rectum, declaring—rather pedantically under the circumstances—"This is definitely worthy of consideration." There is one program which consists of relentless close-ups of a nail-bitten finger sliding in and out of a rectum ringed with coarse black hairs.

On the last channel I discover a program called HOW TO ENLARGE YOUR PENIS. Although it's only an advertisement for *The Stryker Penis Pump,* this show thrills me. With *GQ* good looks and the right combination of acting talent and narcissism, Jeff Stryker has clearly lost himself inside the fantasy. Narrating in dulcet tones, he vacuums his penis along a plexiglass tube with a hand pump. "Look how *big* it is. Look how *thick* it is," he intones, gazing at the contents of the tube as though he has trapped an exotic butterfly there.

1150 COMMRICAL DRIVE

Dogs

George Tyler is driving east on Hastings Street with a dead cat in the trunk of his 1974 Toyota Celica. Low compression, rusting floor panels, blue smoke, no heat, no wipers; the car is on its last legs. It runs continually gas-rich because George is under the false impression that the manual choke button is a defective cigarette lighter.

George is a big pudding of a man, already spilling from his clothing at the age of thirty-one. An alcoholic, like his mother and father and wife, George can't drink any more. But he smokes dope like a fiend. Four or five joints, starting in the early afternoon. Never had as much as a thousand dollars in the bank; he'll be a rent-payer until the day he dies.

George curves left onto the Barnet Highway. The traffic flows easily. The tops of the trees are bathed in orange. He pulls off just west of the rifle range and picks a gravesite halfway up the mountain, close to a razor-wire fence.

George swings the shovel through the slash, preparing a circle of fresh earth, perhaps three feet in diameter. It's very good earth, moist and reddish, ready to be plundered. He stops to rest, leaning on the shovel, panting, gazing from the corners of his eyes as if he is performing mathematical tasks inside his head.

He sits with his feet in the grave, tearing at the box. It is a small, cream-coloured cat with a ringed tail like a raccoon. George examines the body of the cat. There are patches of fur missing from both front paws and dried blood on the teeth and gums. George sits for a long time stroking the stiff cat, running his hands over the face and flanks. A flea crawls out from the cold body.

When he arrives home he finds his two-year-old daughter marching around the house, waving a piece of string, trying to entice the nonexistent cat into a game of chase.

"The cat is gone," George says to his daughter.

"Kitty, kitty, kitty," says George's daughter, trolling with the string along the base of the couch.

George holds his daughter at arm's length, shaking her gently, noticing with displeasure that she is shitting into her diapers as he does this.

"Could you change her?" shouts his wife from the kitchen a moment later.

"I'm tired," says George. "I've just buried the cat."

They eat macaroni and cheese at the kitchen table. The little girl is being difficult, whimpering and not eating.

"The 79-cent dinner," says George, smacking his lips together dramatically.

"It's got extra cheese," says his wife.

"The 89-cent dinner," says George, repeating the gesture with less effect.

They fall into silence. The child inverts her bowl of macaroni and soils herself again before the meal is over.

In bed at night George and his wife lie side by side, breathing shallowly.

"It's just as well that cat got hit," says George's wife.

"Now, why would you say a thing like that?" says George. He turns to her, frowning.

"I'm not really sure why I said that," says his wife.

The next day on his way home from work George stops at the SPCA. In cage after cage, the cats lie passively on sheets of soggy newspaper, sleeping or staring beyond him with half-closed eyes. Either they have given up or they misunderstand their circumstance.

As George retraces his steps along the rows of cages, a fluffy ginger cat totters up to him, sniffing at him through the mesh. George sniffs back. The cat raises itself on its hind legs. He takes the cat home.

"What do you think you're doing?" says George's wife, her gaze fixed on the explosion of orange fluff jittering its way across the kitchen table.

George eats alone at the kitchen table while his wife works methodically on a stack of dirty dishes. There is a cry from the bedroom and he removes the girl from the crib, feeling a wave of resentment as her body stiffens to his touch.

"She only wants her mommy when she's waking up," says George, embarrassed, holding the child out to his wife.

"Let me at least get these gloves off," says George's wife.

She lifts her sweater up and puts the child onto her breast.

"She's almost too old for that," says George.

He goes to the living room and turns the TV on to the hockey game. It's the Canucks vs. the Detroit Red Wings. First televised game of the season. A nothing game. But it's hockey. The big men. Trigger men. Punch-up artists. The orange cat emerges from under the sofa.

"Here kitty, here kitty," says George.

"Kitty, kitty, kitty," says George's daughter, emerging from the kitchen with a piece of banana. She advances on the cat, falls to her knees and traps it against the floor, licking the cat steadily between the ears as if it is an ice cream cone.

"Oh honey, you've got to see this," calls George from the living room.

"What? What is it?" says George's wife, arranging her swollen breasts under the sweater.

"Look at the cat. She's licking the cat."

"Oh Christ," says George's wife, scooping the child up, pushing the cat away. She turns to George. "You know, you're a liability around here."

"What are you talking about?" says George.

"You just sit there while the child is licking the cat."

"I don't see any harm in it."

"You stupid, fat, stoned idiot. That cat probably has fleas and mites."

George's wife retreats to the kitchen holding the crying child under her arm like a bag of groceries.

"Well I'm all you've got, so there," shouts George after her.

"And you just sit there," she says, standing in the doorway.

"That's right," says George.

"You don't help around here," she says.

"That's right," says George, picking up the cat.

"Your daughter can't stand you," she says.

"That's probably right too," says George, placing the cat on his lap.

"You don't even fuck me any more," she says.

"I don't?" says George, genuinely surprised.

"My God, you treat that cat better than me," she says.

"I do like the cat," says George, rubbing his hands carefully through the soft orange fur.

Ancient Mariner Dog Grooming

6437 MAIN STREET
PHONE: 325-6422
SMALL DOGS: $32. SHEPARDS: $45
AFGHANS AND LARGE COLLIES: FROM $50

Rows of yapping dogs in cages and two wide-eyed women. It's hard for me to explain I'm interested in dog grooming, but they believe me because it's true.

A poodle stands shivering on a table with a leather noose around its neck and Linda has a pair of clippers in her hand, soothing the dog as if it is a child waiting for a minor operation.

The basic grooming routines are as follows:

CUTTING: Cutting, or *roughing in,* is just what it sounds like. The idea is to get rid of as much excess hair as possible before the dog is bathed.

BATHING: The dog gets washed in chemical water. It makes him smell better and kills the fleas.

DRYING: You pump a bunch of warm air into his cage to dry him off. This doesn't kill him.

CLIPPING: After the dog has been dried, he is clipped into final shape with a pair of electric clippers. As with your own hair stylist, you are welcome to request the style and extent of the cut.

NAILS: Uncut dog nails will become uncomfortable for the dog and cause damage to your carpets and furniture. In clipping the nails it is vital that you clip only the ends off and do not cut into the vein running down the body of the nail. An amateur should not attempt this stunt. Nothing is more depressing than a dog moving silently over your kitchen floor leaving a trail of bloody footprints.

EARS: This is a somewhat controversial area of dog grooming. If you lift up a dog's ear you will find a bunch of fluffy hair protruding from the ear cavity. Some veterinarians say the hair is needed to protect the inner ear from pollutants, while another school of veterinarians says it does nothing but collect germs. It's one of those things you could argue about for hours and hours.

ANAL GLANDS: This is scary stuff. Each dog has a pair of anal glands. The location, as suggested by the name, is around the anus. The anal glands excrete a brown mucus which functions as a lubricant for exiting feces, and also is released as a signal of submission during a fight. Because of inbreeding, many small dogs have difficulty releasing this fluid. No doubt some of us have seen frustrated pets attempting to drain the glands by dragging themselves across the living room floor on their front paws. When this fails, the dog must be depressurized by hand. As the two pretty dog groomers readily admit, if dog grooming has one blatant professional drawback, it is the assumption of this responsibility.

I feel sorry for dogs. But dogs have an easier time than sheep, who are sheared so brutally that when it's over, it looks as if some weakling has spent an afternoon slashing them with a blunt machete. And some of the old ones just die from the shock. If I come back on a planet with millions of animals more intelligent than me, I hope they are happy, good-hearted creatures.

Kathy's Poodle Palace

(NOW PAWS & CLAWS PET GROOMING)
4938 JOYCE ROAD. PHONE: 434-8222
SMALL DOGS: $35. SHEPHERDS: $40
LARGE COLLIES: $55. AFGHANS: FROM $50

I'm jammed up in a phone booth, all sweaty under the arms, with the horrible feeling of being a nuisance. Good phone conversations are rare at the best of times, but this one is an unqualified disaster. When I say, "May I please speak to Kathy?" it's as if I'm a moron because I don't know that no one at Kathy's Poodle Palace is called Kathy. I can hear the dogs barking behind the brittle female voice. She tells me her name is Melody and she asks me who I am and what I am doing. The conversation terminates abruptly when I ask if I can come round and watch her groom a dog. She says, "Look, I'm sorry. I'm busy. Goodbye." And the click of that phone in my ear is irritating.

Two days later I jam myself up in another phone booth on Kingsway and I dial her number. There's a bald guy riding a bicycle down the shoulder of the road. I see a tundra of ginger hair sprouting from his back, and a pair of plastic bags drooping from the handlebars. Melody is annoyed. I feel as if I'm trying to delay alimony payments or gain access to her teenage daughters. We have the same conversation we had before. Finally she says, "Well I'm sorry, but I'm too busy to talk to you."

So the next day I drop by uninvited, with notebook in hand. It's the first time I've ever been pushy with a stranger. Tap the chrome bell with an index finger and try not to slouch. She's a short woman with peroxide blonde hair and sparkly blue eyes. Not nearly as hard as I pictured her. I say, "Excuse me for dropping by like this," and she looks almost pleased, like I am an old boyfriend who maybe wasn't such a bad guy after all.

There's a little dog with flat teeth, noosed on a small circular table. If he jumps he'll break his neck or twist it most painfully.

SALSBURY AND EAST 1ST AVENUE

Melody says this is a Lhaso, a Tibetan dog, the kind of dog that'll sneak up on you and start humping your leg when you are trying to say something important. She says they're one of the hardest breeds of dog to clip because the front legs turn outward as if the dog has spent its entire life running on ice. It's so seldom I get to sit alone with a woman and watch her clip a dog.

And Melody has won grooming competitions. I'm scribbling stuff on the notepad to show a degree of competence. I say, "I heard that fleas are actually good for dogs." She stops clipping and turns to face me with the pretty blue eyes: "Fleas are good for dogs. That's a good one. I'll have to remember that one."

Pets Beautiful by Jeannine

5589 DUNBAR (AT 40TH)
PHONE: 261-5310
HOURS: TUES–SAT: 8.30 A.M.–4:30 P.M.
SPANIEL: $25. RETRIEVER: $25. POODLE: $50

I'm way up here in Waspland where some people say the women out shopping are just single-client prostitutes with household management skills. When you see them stooping for the big bag of Canada Fancy frozen peas, they look tired and resentful as if no amount of payment could fully compensate for the indignity. When I have a wife, I intend to fall in love with her and hire someone I don't love to go stooping through the frozen stuff. Life is short so we won't bother snipping out all kinds of coupons just to save a couple of pennies.

Jeannine is a stout middle-aged woman with quick girlish movements. She is cutting a spaniel, showing me the matted fur on the dog's ears and explaining that the owner deceived her—told her the fur was combed and untangled. She says, "I've been here nineteen years," and she freezes, as if this has never occurred to her before, " . . . almost twenty years . . . it's hard to believe. I'm sure I don't know where they've gone." The dogs stare at me from their cages against the wall.

There are two assistants working in the background. One is a pale Englishman named Marcus who came to B.C. some years ago from the outskirts of London. He's hosing down a terrier in a bathtub raised two feet off the ground. The terrier stands rigidly in front of him. Marcus says, "I wash them all exactly the same way and that way I don't miss anything." The dog jumps crisply out of the tub and shakes itself dry on a wooden platform flush with the top of the tub.

Marcus buys a coffee. He says, "It's actually no worse in the south of England than it is here. All my English relatives are working and the same can't be said of their Canadian counterparts."

The other assistant, Paulette, is a shy pudding of a girl, bent over a white miniature poodle. The poodle is old, shaking violently as the clippers run along the skin around its paws. When I ask, Paulette tells me about herself in quick sentences that flow together urgently, as if she is afraid I may lose interest while she is speaking. She was born in Langley, raised in Richmond, Surrey and Burnaby. Her parents met in Vancouver. Her mother was brought up by Catholic nuns in an orphanage in Paris. Jeannine was also brought up by Catholic nuns. This is how she describes it:

> Well, I have five brothers and no sisters. When I turned twelve my mother suddenly realized she had a daughter. I honestly don't think it occurred to her until that moment. It really surprised her. I mean, she treated us all the same up to that point. Anyway, off I went to a convent at the age of twelve. Do you know what they said to my mother the first day I arrived? "Don't worry, we'll break her." Six years I was there and they never broke me. What monsters.

> Oh, I did miss my brothers. I was used to being spoiled and pampered by them and then suddenly, there I was with 300 girls. Girls! I didn't know the first thing about girls. I didn't trust them. They seemed false, scheming, hypocritical. Boys are trained to—well, they just say what they feel. I guess that's it. Boys are very simple and obvious in that way. If something is bothering them, they just, say it. But a girl will pout for a week. [trying a pout] You don't know where you stand with them. I still think they're a weird bunch.

> You started the month with ten merit points. Every time you did something wrong you lost a couple of points, and you lost some privileges, like going on walks into town. We used to love that. Going to town in our uniforms. Black stockings. Black dress. Pink silk on the inside, and pleats here on the chest, and down here in front there was a big pocket, like a kangaroo pouch.

Anything private had to go in that pouch. I'd keep all my love letters right in there. It was the one place they couldn't touch.

I remember the hardest time was in the spring. Past the orchard I could see the town kids walking home from school. In fact they all seemed to be skipping. And oh my! Some of them would be holding hands. Can you imagine how I felt? I'd look out there and think to myself, "Will I ever get out of here? Will I ever be normal?"

[to the spaniel] You're not setting a very good example. Be still, you. [to Marcus] Yes I'll have a coffee. In fact, that's all I'll have. I'm dieting today. I stepped on the scales last night, and oh my God! I've been a naughty girl.

MARCUS: It was probably that luncheon we had.
JEANNINE: I think you're right.
MARCUS: We ate lunch at the Delta Inn.
JEANNINE: All you can eat for $12.95.
MARCUS: We pigged out.
JEANNINE: I couldn't help it. There were cheeses and cakes and pies and shrimp. Tables and tables of food, and we just sat there with a bottle of wine, looking out at the boats on the river. I put eight oysters on my plate.
MARCUS: You would've taken more if the waiter hadn't been watching.
JEANNINE: That's true. You're right. I would've taken more. And as a bonus, there was an opera singer, singing at a birthday party for a ninety-year-old woman. Singing in Italian or Latin or something.
MARCUS: I think it was Italian.
JEANNINE: Italian.
MARCUS: [quietly] It was a good afternoon.
JEANNINE: Yes it certainly was.
MARCUS: . . . by the river.
JEANNINE: It was a beautiful afternoon.

3561 MAIN STREET

At Pets Beautiful I confirmed a suspicion that dog grooming is labour intensive, and the standard charge of $25–$50 per dog works out to a very reasonable hourly rate. Although they are not flashy in a technical sense, Jeannine, Marcus and Paulette may be depended on to work through every step of the operation with meticulous care, producing a clean attractive dog.

B.C. Pet Cemetery

14735–76TH AVENUE, SURREY
PHONE: 596-3635
BURIAL: $150–$400

I'm totally lost. Even with a map and lots of advice from the natives, I'm going around in circles. I think this is the trick to Surrey's expansionism: a guy gets so desperately lost he just gives up and buys a piece of land to settle on. I see a conspiracy of scraggly youths hanging around the 7-Eleven, smoking pot and giving each other a feel. If I was going to live here that's exactly what I'd like to spend my time doing.

It took only four hours of my day to get here. This is practically farm land. I can see them peeking at me from behind the curtains as I walk up the drive. I must admit I'm dressed like a fool. Pajamas and black leather boots would probably raise an eyebrow in the best of circumstances. The woman who answers the door is older than my mother. She looks like a grandmother. Her name is Roberta Bateson.

GUY: Hi! Can I see the cemetery?

ROBERTA: [worried] Well, yes you may, but, did you have something you wanted buried?

GUY: Yes I did.

ROBERTA: A dog, a cat?

GUY: A dog.

ROBERTA: Oh dear. Is it, well, dead?

GUY: No, but it is very sick. It has dog cancer.

ROBERTA: Oh dear. Well, you know, we can't, you know, bury anything now.

GUY: Why not?

ROBERTA: [more worried] Well, our gravediggers have the flu. They're very sick. Just young boys, well, like you. I don't know what to do. We've had four phone calls about dogs this morning. I'm just looking after the place. Mrs. Blair is in charge of it. She's my aunt. She's in the hospital.

GUY: Can I dig my own hole?

ROBERTA: Well, yes, you may. That would be a good idea. The cemetery is round back. Drive to the end of the dirt road, past all the houses, right past all the houses, you'll see it there at the end of the road. Well, that's where it is.

It's a beautiful little plot of land, surrounded by tall pine trees and a chickenwire fence. It starts to rain. I linger in the car letting the warm air shoot up the leg of my pajamas. I find a grave with a baseball on it and the stone sculpture of a poodle. Ice crystals gather together and point out of the broken earth. I see the words Mommy and Daddy written all over these tombstones.

Our beloved baby Fluffy
We miss you
Mommy and Daddy and Patsy
March 7 '55 – October 12 '70

An elderly couple climb out of a brown Buick. The man is carrying a whisk broom and the woman has a bouquet of flowers. They open the chickenwire gate and step gingerly across the frozen grass, stopping by a flat grave in the middle of the cemetery. There are two dogs in one grave: Sailor and Skipper. The woman smiles at me and says, "I don't come out as much as I used to because I've been in an accident. It's hard now. But I miss my old girl, and the little one too." I say, "Do you have another dog now?" and she shakes her head sadly as she sweeps the surface of the grave.

If you are planning to bury your dog in a pet cemetery, you should be aware of additional costs incurred in the purchase of a gravestone and concrete border. The actual burial fee is computed on the basis of weight, a poodle running about $150 and large Shepherd around $400. The complete cost, including a gravestone, could easily run close to a thousand dollars.

Death

I used to sit with my mother and father and watch the evening news, maps of Vietnam, bloodshed, the lottery, and the hockey scores.

I kept a large white rat in my bedroom. With no excess of imagination, I named him Ben. I liked him more than a boy probably should like a rat. I fed him lettuce and toast and let him bury the tip of his nose deep into my ear. All kinds of new people dropped by to play with my rat.

When the summer came I trained him to sit on my shoulder while I rode my bicycle. We rode all over the neighbourhood and everywhere we went people wrinkled their noses and said, "Is that a *rat* on your shoulder?" In the supermarket one woman actually screamed. It was a weird ugly one that rose like a siren and then got choked up in her throat somewhere. By the end of the summer Ben's teeth were long and curved and yellow like my beaver teeth. I stopped wetting my toothbrush to fool my mother.

One night when I fell asleep reading, Ben crawled into bed with me and bit my private parts. It was the only time he ever bit me. I examined myself under a light. When I saw that the skin wasn't punctured, I decided not to tell anyone.

The next day it rained. All it did was rain. I was more bored than I'd ever been in my life. I dropped Ben into a sink of warm water. He didn't like it. He swam around in silent circles, scratching the sides of the sink with his tiny paws. I pushed him under the water and watched the bubbles stream up out of his nose. After a while he slowed down and I pulled him out and placed him on a fluffy white towel. He just lay there shivering.

I plugged in my sister's blow dryer and poured hot air onto him, making sure to keep the nozzle away from him. He dragged himself off the towel using only his front paws. I brought him a chunk of cheddar cheese, a big one, which he would normally have tried to haul back into his cage. He sniffed and stared up at me without moving. I took him upstairs. My mother said, "Ben has had a stroke."

That night I lay awake empty and scared. When I woke Ben was crouching dead in his cage. His eyes pointed downward, as if he were concentrating on his toes. I dug a hole and buried him in the back garden. My mother said, "He was very sweet, very special. He had a good life." I thought about the bubbles and said a prayer for him.

What followed was a week of crying despair. My pain was probably diminished by the fact that he was, after all, only a rat, and intensified by the knowledge that I had been the sole cause of his death, either through deliberate cruelty, or at the very least, ground-breaking stupidity. Now, what does my book have to say about the needs of the human heart? Sadly, almost nothing.

Once, when my heart was broken, I swam a mile every day. After swimming I felt some relief.

Perhaps a quick review of the history of the world might be useful. The earth, they figure, is about 2,000 million years old. For 1,700 million years it was lifeless. Man has existed as "a self-conscious social creature" for thirty thousand years, and the frisbee has been here for twenty. These facts provide a useful framework for your grief. A lot of stuff has been dying on this planet for a long time and you simply must accept the dwarfish nature of your own concerns. My sister thinks this is a lousy argument. She says, "Guy, that's ridiculous; if I hook an electrode up to your testicles and pour five hundred volts into you, does the pain go away when I tell you there are a million other men hooked up that way?" I think I can state, without fear of contradiction, that that's a typical thing for her to say. She's always right. Everything about her is right. She owns her own car. She plays the violin. Her breasts hold firm without a bra. She beats me in Scrabble. Her baby shits English toffee and never cries except to release tension. You know it really bugs me when

one person thinks they're better than another person just because they happen to be born before the other person. They
forget that means they'll probably die first.

Armstrong & Company Funeral Directors

304 DUNLEVY AVENUE
PHONE: 254-7166

I'm still panting from the bicycle ride, so it looks pretty dramatic when I burst onto the Persian rugs and blurt out an unforgivable lie: "My mother's dead!"

Find myself ushered into a private room with Chinese art on the walls. They send in a white guy even though there's nothing but Orientals running around in the hallways. Pull myself together and shake his hand, stoically. He's impressed. There's always the suggestion of a military background in this ability to suppress emotion under pressure. He asks, "Where is her body now?" Oops. I can see that a lie is like a living thing, no sooner has it arrived in the world than it wants to start producing more of itself. I say, "Kelowna," and he says, "I'm afraid, Mr. Bennett, there will be extra costs involved in transporting her from Kelowna."

I give a special wave of my hand that shows impatience and a batsqueak of amusement. Cost is not the issue here. I tell him I would like to see the chapel, where all her friends may come to view the body, and a member of the clergy may be hired to recite some words. He says, "I must warn you, Mr. Bennett, it really is a very small chapel." I hurry through it, past the shiny pews painted yellow, and along to the casket room—increasingly uncomfortable as we build a house on the foundation of this ugly lie.

He says, "Most of our clients are Chinese, and they will spend a great deal on a nice casket." Well, let's look at the most expensive one you've got. Christ, do I really look like such an

200 BLOCK WEST BROADWAY

ass as to drop a thing like that into the ground and cover it with earth? Let me out of here. I'm glad I told so many lies as a kid because it's no fun now.

Chapel of Chimes

55 EAST 10TH AVENUE
PHONE: 876-8877

It's like a New England ancestral home, with the flickering gas fireplace and the soft grey wall-to-wall carpeting. I can hear a man on the phone to his stockbroker. Never break this habit of eavesdropping; maybe pick up some tips and make an investment myself. A box of kleenex on every rosewood table. Peel one off and honk my sinuses into it.

Nothing to do but gaze around the room, take in all the artwork. I'm quite capable of appreciating a lot of this drab historical stuff, although I still prefer my blacklight posters. Here's an interesting one: bustling medieval courtyard with smartly dressed servants packing trunks into a horse-drawn coach, sniffing dogs and fluttering chickens. There's a pretty maid waving a silk hankie from the courtyard balcony. She looks radiant and mischievous, full of life. And yet I read they were a lice-ridden bunch who never bathed or used deodorants. I'd have to search out a passive creature, perhaps some working class beauty, teach her the rituals of modern hygiene—explain it as a deep-rooted personal perversion, leave no room for discussion or compromise.

Ushered up the stairs into a spacious room dotted with Edwardian furniture. Sit down at a desk big enough to seat ten IBM typists. Thank God I changed out of my jungle boots. The conversation turns to death. There are many interruptions because on this particular day, the secretary has gone home early. The stockbroker calls back. He is told, "Listen, I'm busy, why don't you just send me a list of the numbers?"

Soft light sprays up into the chapel from tulip-shaped lights on either side of the pulpit. The wooden pews are oiled and polished. Voices disappear, blown away like dust at the moment of their release. It has the feel of a church built by a rich man in a small town. The balcony section, originally built to accommodate overflow, is never used these days because, as the town has

1206 COMMERCIAL DRIVE

grown, community spirit has dwindled; attendance at funerals is always low.

The chapel spills out into a lounge area flooded with natural pale blue light. Two long black mats running over the cement mark the route of the hearse, which is driven *inside* the building. It's exciting: the thought of a shiny American-made car gobbled up inside a funeral home, hot pistons pounding away under the hood, noxious fumes mixing with the sad memories and the platitudes of death. Beyond the concrete is a spacious carpeted area, empty except for one pale plastic green fern with delicate painted leaves.

The price structure of a funeral service at the Chapel of Chimes is much the same as other funeral homes covered in this book. Physically, this is the most attractive funeral home I've been in. And, perhaps, through the confidence that comes with this knowledge, the personnel is more relaxed, less smarmy. When I thanked the man for showing me around, he shook my hand warmly and said, "Please don't call me Mister. It's Don. Don. You make me feel old."

Forest Lawn Funeral Home

FOREST LAWN MEMORIAL PARK
3789 ROYAL OAK, BURNABY.
PHONE: 299-7720

Ushered along the dark wooden corridors of the funeral home, I'm amazed to find myself simultaneously flatulent and aroused. There's just the sound of our feet and these rooms are big enough to play soccer in.

Meet Assistant Manager Geoff Bleasby, a middle-aged English gentleman with a slightly embalmed look, enhanced, no doubt, by long hours of dedication to a job that provides little opportunity for power tanning and checking out the beach bunnies. Mr. Bleasby got right to the point. "We are not all rich," he said, "and money is often an issue." We proceeded to talk business.

Full Funeral Service at $2,360 includes:

—removal of the body
—embalming
—paperwork
—evening visitation prior to funeral
—the funeral service

It does not include:

—minister's fee ($150-250)
—death certificate ($20)
—flowers ($100 and up)
—casket ($1,200 and up)
—gravestone ($200 and up)
—gravesite ($200 and up)
—organist ($65)
—hair ($35)

Now if, as Mr. Bleasby suggested, money is an issue, there are several cheaper ways to dispose of oneself. One is a $675 Graveside Service, where the deceased lies inside the casket unavailable for public viewing. After some religious gesturing, the body is dropped straight into the ground. All the additional expenses incurred with the Full Funeral Service apply to the graveside service, so basically you save yourself some money by not having the body dolled up.

Mr. Bleasby gave me a tour of his casket room. Much the same stuff, but this time a $6,000 bronze casket, very popular with the Chinese, he says. When all is said and done, the cheapest and most practical way to go is still an old-fashioned burning. With no casket, gravestone or cemetery plot to worry about, the whole thing will run you about $1,380, leaving you with a pile of ashes. Spreading ashes is littering and therefore strictly illegal, but hells bells, who's going to know? Rent a helicopter and toss them out over the Rockies.

Roselawn Funeral Chapel

1669 EAST BROADWAY

PHONE: 879-6821

This is the way I'd have my billiard room done, with lots of rosewood and paper cylinders covering the naked bulbs. Always feel a smile coming on around the trappings of death. A nervous false one like when you want to get laid at a party.

It's down to business without a handshake. I'd like to pre-arrange my mother's funeral. My mother is a bull. Don't look startled, it's an image for her stubbornness. She refuses to come and talk to you. Let's just us talk. Put away those forms why don't you?

I don't know her faith. She never mentioned it. I think a humanistic service sounds bang on. I'll give the eulogy myself and make every other eye wet by keeping mine dry. An important tip for young actors, that. Eleven hundred and ninety five dollars includes the family limousine. Yes, well it would have to when you consider; that amount of money represents a month in Mexico away from this disgusting drizzle.

That's a hell of a suit he's wearing there, and it helps me believe him when he says, "There's absolutely no pressure to buy anything. All the decisions belong to you and your mother." I'll think of him as a friendly helper. It's the McDonald's ethic without all those pimply fifteen-year-olds who never wink back at me.

THE TOUR OF THE CASKET ROOM:

> Have you ever been inside a casket room before, Guy? No? Well, it's different. There's every kind of casket you can think of. This is a $2,500 steel casket with a mono-seal to keep the bugs out. Fifty-year guarantee, useful if there is any question of disinterment, like the Greeks who are so often removed from the ground and taken

back to Greece after the burial. You've got fifty years to make that decision. It may seem strange to you, but a lot of people care very much what happens to the body after the funeral. The Chinese particularly will go for these steel caskets, or the copper ones over here, which are absolutely the best caskets you can buy in terms of protecting the body from worms and so forth. Of course, the body still decomposes but at least there are no bugs running around in there. Okay, this is nothing more than a cardboard box, for Direct Cremation only. It sells for $30. The body may not be viewed in this box. I have it in the showroom only because . . . well, if someone is going to be so cheap . . . I shouldn't say cheap. Let's put it this way: if someone has no more respect for their mother than they would a dog, then I have to sell them the box. You see, the whole point is, it's not what I want that matters, it's what you want. It's something that you're doing for your mother and, when you think about it, for yourself as well. It will be very important to look back and know that you did everything you could . . . feel this! This is octagonal design wooden box . . . a smaller model for a child or an older person. A smaller older person would look swamped in that copper casket, but they would look very attractive—well, attractive—I shouldn't say attractive—what I mean is, you'll be able to recognize the person and they'll seem comfortable. They'll look as if they are resting in peace, and later on, that'll be important, so that you can remember them that way.

ORGAN DONATION

By all means be an organ donor, but I would warn you against leaving your body to medical science in an unqualified fashion. You are liable to end up on a slab with your veins and arteries pumped full of plastic, surrounded by a gaggle of barely post-adolescent medical students. They'll cut you into ribbons and pass bits of you around saying stuff like: "Let me give you a hand here," and "Jeez, I'm all thumbs today," and finally at the

97

2195 COMMERCIAL DRIVE

end of the year one of the fraternity boys might grate you into a dormitory salad or stir somebody's drink with you. It's a long tough road on this twirling ball of puddles and dirt, and you don't want to end up as a prop in somebody's sick joke.

Miscellaneous

On the day she entered high school Carla was already six feet tall. She had pale skin, wide cheekbones and ocean-green eyes which darted around inside her head as if they were seeking a way out. Her hair was thick and black. It ran straight down her back to her buttocks, like Oriental hair. Her breasts were firm and full without being large. She played piano beautifully. She had poise. Her peers were intimidated.

Carla lived alone with her father. He was a sad figure, a commercial artist whose finest achievement was a woodcut, *Child on Rollerskates*—a piece he created ripped on acid in his second year of college. He didn't speak much, and when he spoke it was mostly about small domestic issues: the temperature of the basement, the flow of water through the gutters, a blade of grass poking a crack in the asphalt driveway. Once, when Carla was only ten, he rubbed soap meticulously over her naked body, saying matter-of-factly, "This is how you do it if you want to be *really* clean." That night he took her out for pizza. There wasn't much to say.

In the spring semester of her first high school year, Carla surrendered her virginity to a dull frizzy-haired kid, a small-time dope dealer, automobile fanatic, a minor figure on the basketball team. She discarded him immediately after the first use and launched into a period of unchecked promiscuity. Her father was not blind to these proceedings. He said, "There are demons inside of you," and sent her to live in Wellington, New Zealand, with her Aunt Sally.

Aunt Sally lived in a quaint wooden house overlooking the

ocean. She taught history at a local university and drank furiously in the evenings. There was a grand piano in the living room. Carla played it. Aunt Sally told her, "There are great things inside you, there are great things in store for you."

One night when Carla got up to urinate, she found a young man floating in the bathtub. He had blonde ringlets falling to his shoulders. He smiled. The water in the tub was grey. He said, "Hello, I'm your cousin John." He extended a hand, and as he did so, his penis rose from the grimy soup like a battered submarine. Carla return to her room with a full bladder.

She awoke as he climbed into bed with her. Very simply, he said, "There's nowhere else to sleep." When Aunt Sally woke she saw the motorcycle helmet and the greasy leather bags in the living room. She found her son in bed with Carla. The covers were thrown back to their ankles. They were fast asleep in the morning sun, tangled like individual strands of spaghetti cooling on the side of a plate.

Aunt Sally was very hurt. She said, "Carla, I want you out of my house."

Carla went home to her father. The demons attacked again.

Arthur Murray School of Dance

695 SMITHE STREET
PHONE: 684-2477
HOURS: MON–FRI: 11 A.M.–10 P.M;
SAT: 11 A.M.–6 P.M.

Back in the 1920s, in New York City, Arthur Murray invented a system of dance instruction centred on the Magic Steps. He opened up shop claiming that he could teach anyone to dance. Over sixty years later there are 250 Arthur Murray Dance Studios around the world. You can phone any one of them and make an appointment for a free introductory lesson, and that is what I did.

My teacher's name is Lola. She is a middle-aged woman, light and bubbly and thin as a rake. Her pants are baggy silky things, so that if you spilled something on them, you'd be there all evening trying to wipe it off. I take off my jacket and we move out onto the wooden dance floor.

GUY: I should warn you, I'm not the world's most physical guy.
LOLA: What kind of dancing would you like to learn?
GUY: I don't really care.
LOLA: Social dancing?
GUY: I want to be respected by my peers.
LOLA: Anything else?
GUY: Yes. Confidence. I need some of that.
LOLA: I'm going to teach you some simple steps. You'll be surprised how easy it is.

There's another couple out here with us. Lola says that is a good thing because it gets you used to the hustle and bustle of social dancing. We hold hands and look in the mirror. Walk forward and backward. Correct the penguin in my gait. Now the waltz. With my arms around her waist. I don't waste any time stepping on her foot. She'll probably have a charley horse and a bad back by the time I'm done. I can feel that I'm being led. It's the first time I've ever waltzed. When my elbows begin to sag she whispers "Spaghetti." We're gliding across the dance floor in lilting circles. She won't let me look into her eyes. I see there is a sign forbidding fraternization between instructors and students. I think we know that love has its own rules.

After learning the rhumba, the swing and the foxtrot, I'm sitting flushed in her office. Lola grades me on my dancing, checking little boxes that say Good, Excellent or Average.

She says I have lots of potential. But it is too early to tell how much. For $170 you can buy a package of 4 one-hour private lessons, 4 one-hour group lessons and 2 practice parties.

LOLA: Will it be cheque or credit card?
GUY: I have to go home and think about it.
LOLA: Oh.
GUY: I'm not quite ready to make a decision.
LOLA: When people want to go home and think, it usually means that there is a question I haven't answered. Do you have any questions?
GUY: Not really.
LOLA: [getting up] Well then, I hope I see you again.

The Magic Steps really do work. They work so well that there is virtually no sales pitch beyond a demonstration of their power in a free half-hour introductory lesson. Lola smells good and she smiles like a lovely old hippie reeling in a fat rainbow trout.

The Young Bride's Shop Ltd.

40–6TH STREET, NEW WESTMINSTER
PHONE: 522-4214
HOURS: MON–THU: 10:00 A.M.–5:30 P.M; FRI:
10 A.M.–9 P.M.

Even though it doesn't usually work, marriage is still popular, and many couples are observing the formal Christian ritual surrounding it.

Choosing a lifetime partner is a very tricky thing, involving concepts and sensibilities slightly beyond the scope of this book, and indeed altogether outside my own areas of expertise. However, I think it is safe to say that when the decision has been made, and the date set, you are going to want to look pretty. If you are pretty, you are going to want to look beautiful. Nothing could be more reasonable. And the first thing to do is choose a stunning wedding dress.

For this assignment I recruited my sister, a saucy redhead just entering her eighth month of pregnancy. She proved to have quite a journalistic eye herself, commenting that in New Westminster everyone parks at an oblique angle to the curb. The woman who served us had long curving yellow fingernails. She glanced down at my sister's swollen belly. We made apologetic noises. The saleswoman said, "Good heavens, people are always so embarrassed about it. They think they're the only ones. It happens all the time. Now, when are you due?"

We looked through racks and racks of wedding dresses. Not all of them were white the way I'd imagined. The saleswoman found us a flashy yellow chiffon dress with an expandable waistline.

SARA: [clasping her hands together] Can we possibly afford it?
GUY: I don't know.
SARA: We could save up.
GUY: Well, how much is it?

200 BLOCK WEST BROADWAY

SALESWOMAN: It's $350, with 15% off that.
GUY: Oh boy.
SARA: [close to tears] Oh Guy!
GUY: I'm sorry.
SARA: You're so cheap.
GUY: All right, try it on then.
SARA: [aside] I don't have underwear on.
GUY AND SARA: [smiling] Look at us. We're walking back-
wards.

As well as an impressive variety of wedding dresses, we found colourful bridesmaid dresses, and an assortment of gaudy wedding paraphernalia, like a heart-shaped white lace cushion to carry the ring on. You can rent bridesmaid dresses for $50 per weekend. I don't recommend you buy a Mother's Gown. To my eye they are bulky, unattractive things. Instead, Mother can be imaginatively and economically outfitted using removable body paint and a family-size roll of Glad Wrap.

Woolworth's

149 WEST HASTINGS
PHONE: 685-6923
HOURS: MON TO FRI: 9:30 A.M.–9 P.M; SAT:
9:30 A.M.–5:30 P.M; SUN: NOON–5 P.M.

Woolworth's is a great store because it has lots of cheap stuff in it. There's so much raw sensuality oozing from the staff that sometimes it's hard to remember what you came for. Here is a short list of Woolworth's products, representative of the entire stock in theme and price.

Earrings:	$ 1.97
2 L Conditioning Rinse:	$ 2.99
6 drinking glasses with jug:	$13.99
Lampshade:	$24.88
Extra Tough Tool Box:	$ 8.00

Many of the products have innovative design features. For instance the tool box comes with "extra tough padlock eye for locking lid to base—also provides convenient way to anchor box on remote job sites!" I find sturdy looking silver oven mitts for $5.77 and a set of Days of the Week 100% acetate panties for $10.96—the latter throwing me into a state of confusion as I distinctly remember from organic chemistry that acetate is a gas at room temperature.

Perhaps the most exciting product is a pair of Posable Modern Army Figures, which are a variation on the g.i. Joes of my youth. Their code names are Tomax and Xamot. They come equipped with a "swivel arm battle grip" and their specialties are "infiltration, espionage, sabotage, propaganda and corporate law." The instructions read as follows: "Spell out the word tomax in capitals and hold it up to a mirror. It reads xamot. The same holds true for the actual brothers. Each is a mirror image of the other except for the scar on Xamot's face." I look carefully and sure enough, one of the the little guys has a tiny red scar on his cheek. Who said shopping at Woolworth's is boring?

4386 MAIN STREET

Shopping at Woolworth's is not boring.

My Woolworth's experience ended in bliss as the muzak programming slipped a cog and they piped in Lou Reed's immortal "Walk on the Wild Side."

Epilogue

When he came back from college, Little Jo was full of himself despite the fact he had failed about half of his subjects. He thought, "This is going to be a great summer," and it was for some people, but not for Little Jo.

As he unpacked his clothes, his mother cooked him a fine dinner of steak, potatoes, peas and salad. She sat across from him, her head cradled in the palm of her hand. Little Jo didn't care if she wanted to watch. The food was good. She said to him, "Little Jo, I wouldn't have believed it possible, but you are even more beautiful than your father was."

After dinner Little Jo excused himself, walked out the back door, opened the garage and threw the canvas cover off his 1973 burgundy Trans Am. It was a beast. A four-barrel, steel-belted, air-conditioned, gas-guzzling monster—a perfectly constructed mechanical slave. When it kicked to life on the first turn of the key, he gave up the idea of tuning it, just climbed in and drove up Orchard Valley, and parked under a grove of plum trees by the lake where he sat and listened to the ticking sounds of the engine cooling. The mosquitoes danced in a layer above the lake. Everything was protected under the orange sky. Little Jo chain-smoked and gazed into the perfect vision of his future.

Five miles away, Astrid the Donut Queen was pouring coffee for two elderly customers, entertaining them by contorting her face to make it look as if it were pressed against the glass, making little piggy sounds. They laughed quietly, glancing at one another, embarrassed because they were so fond of her. Little Jo pulled the Trans Am into the parking space in front of the Donut Shop. "He's back," the Donut Queen observed. When he tried to kiss her she pushed him away as if he were the family dog about to be put to sleep. She said "Little Jo, things have changed." He called a few minutes later from a telephone booth, asking her, "What do you want?" "Nothing but space," she said.

Little Jo felt bad. He went home and slept for eleven hours. When he got up he made a practical decision: he must go on living. He went to see his uncle. Every summer he worked for his uncle, welding boat trailers in a manufacturing plant. The Uncle hugged him and said, "I'm sorry, Little Jo, business is way down. Layoffs. No afternoon shift. I've got a job on the paint line if you want it."

Working on the paint line was the most strenuous job in the factory. It was hard and it was repetitive. Seven and a quarter hours feeding an overhead conveyor belt, hoisting up 15-pound shelving units, suspending them on hooks which dangled at face level. And everything worked on a twelve second cycle. Every twelve seconds, another 15-pound unit, another set of hooks. The men on the paint line were muscular and vacant, breathing in the fumes from the acid bath next to the paint booth. Little Jo said, "Forget it."

He went to a bar, sat on a bar stool drinking beer, ignoring the barmaid, the pool table, the noise of the jukebox. When the bar closed he climbed into the Trans Am and drove it out onto the highway, took it up to 100 mph, eventually crashing into a concrete lane divider, tumbling head over heels inside the metal box. Little Jo stepped out unharmed. The attending officer was an old buddy of his. No breathalyzer. The Trans Am was written off. Little Jo walked away with a cheque for $5,000 and he immediately jumped on a plane for N.Y.C.

It took him six days to blow the money on whores, cocaine and booze. He flew home and went to work on the paint line. One morning his mother brought him a letter from college. It was already opened. Her eyes were sad, almost unbelieving. Little Jo flunked out. He was not eligible to return to college.

Little Jo worked on the paint line for three more years. His body grew strong. He took up amateur boxing. After ten fights he was 5–5–0. He quit boxing. On a whim, he took a job in a muffin shop. Much to his surprise, he like baking. The shop expanded into pies, quiches, sausage rolls, and cakes. When the opportunity arose, Little Jo bought the business and renamed it *Little Jo's*. Two years later he used it as collateral to buy a small house.

Everything was there but the wife and the 1.7 kids. Sure enough, Little Jo married a travel agent named Susan. She was a bit dim, but pretty, in a straightforward way, as her name suggests. Their first child was a boy: a happy, perfectly proportioned lad with curly black hair and watery brown eyes. They were thrilled. They had two more boys.

When the oldest boy was just starting elementary school, Little Jo discovered a roll of fat on his stomach. He didn't like it, didn't like what it represented. He began jogging before going to work. One day, among bills, he found a red envelope in his mailbox. Inside was a short letter from Astrid the Donut Queen. She was travelling through Europe, doing promotion for a perfume company. There was a photo of her sitting on a brick wall in front of a beach. She was pointing at the camera, making a pig face. At the bottom of the card there was a lipstick imprint of her beautiful Swedish lips, slightly parted.

Susan was shaving her legs in the bathtub. A basketball bounced in the driveway. The air was filled with the shrill competitive voices of his sons. Little Jo stared at the card dumbly. He couldn't help feeling there was something inappropriate about the imprint of those lips, on that card, after all this time.

EAST 28TH AND MAIN STREET

THE AUTHOR:

Guy Bennett lives with a muscular brunette and two children in a house with a truss roof.

THE PHOTOGRAPHER:

Mandelbrot takes pictures for Geist magazine.